I AM
WIDOW,
HEAR ME
ROAR

CONFESSIONS OF A
SURVIVING SPOUSE

JOANN KUZMA DEVENY

Other books by JoAnn Kuzma Deveny

When Bluebirds Fly: Losing a Child, Living with Hope

99 Ways to Make a Flight Attendant Fly —Off the Handle!
A Guide for the Novice or Oblivious Air Traveler

I AM WIDOW, HEAR ME ROAR

CONFESSIONS OF A SURVIVING SPOUSE

JOANN KUZMA DEVENY

2018
Fly High Books
Mound, Minnesota

Fly High Books
5017 Wilshire Blvd.
Mound, MN 55364

www.joanndeveny.com
Please contact for quantity discounts and permissions.

Printed in the United States of America

Deveny, JoAnn Kuzma
I Am Widow, Hear Me Roar: Confessions of a Surviving Spouse
Issued also as an eBook.

ISBN-13: 978-0-692-17655-9
1. Widow—Psychological aspects. 2. Widow humor. 3. Widow—Faith.
4. Child Bereavement. 5. Spiritualism.

Library of Congress: 2018909485

First Edition

Cover design by EM Graphics, LLC and Fuzion Print
Cover photo and all other photos by JoAnn Deveny

In memory of Dick,
who was the definition of a loving husband.

In memory of Jennie,
who surpassed the loving definition of a mother.

Table of Contents

1. *My Transformation* | 1

2. *Labor Day and Chicken Noodle Soup:* | 5
   September 2002

3. *Vacations, Coffee Mugs and Cheap Jewelry* | 7

4. *A Grief Remembered and* | 13
   Four-Year-Old Wisdom

5. *The Hospital—Wednesday* | 17

6. *Romeo, Romeo, Wherefore Art Thou...Dick?* | 19

7. *The Hospital—Thursday* | 23

8. *Confessions: Not So Sweet* | 27

9. *The Hospital—Friday* | 31

10. *Confessions: Thou Shall Take His Name in Vain* | 35

11. *The Coffee Was Always Ready* | 37

12. *A Stand-In Dad—and a Racoon* | 43

13. *A Mute Teenager and Borrowed Tears* | 47

14. *Confessions: The Regretful Closet* | 51

15. *Spirits, Loons and Roses* | 55

16. *Confessions: A Fair-Weather* | 59
    Friend Named Denial

17. *Then There Were Two* | 61

18. *Friends and the Lonely Pariah* | 65

19. *Confessions: Helicopters and a Football Mom* | 69

20. *Where's That Brawny Guy and* | 73
    His Allen Wrenches?

21. *Confessions: Booze and Embarrassment* | 77

22. *Wanted and Unwanted Dreams* | 81

23. *Lava Lamps and Robbers* | 85

24. *Chandeliers and a Church Lady* | 89

25. *Confessions: The Apple Doesn't* | 93
    Fall Far from the Tree

26. *Unanswered and Unasked Questions* | 97

27. *Bah-Humbug* | 99

28. *True Blue and New* | 103

29. *Holidays Will Kill You* | 105

30. *Confessions: First Dance and One Last Beer* | 109

31. *The Real Dick (Pardon the Pun)* | 113

32. *Pee Wee and Cathartic Cocktail Napkins* | 117

33. *College and Meds for Moms* | 121

34. *Grow Old with Me, Please* | 125

35. *The Produce Guy, His Wife, and a Gun* | 129

36. *We're Not a Match* | 133

37. *38 First Dates* | 137

38. *Confessions: Bravery and Brain Injuries* | 141

39. *Blind Dates and Dick Van Dyke* | 145

40. *Crazy (Can't Blame It on the Cat) Ladies* | 147

41. *Christmas Letters and a Crutch* | 153

42. *Confessions: Mowing Forward* | 159

Epilogue: *Perception and the Colors of Healing* | 163

The Devenys (photo album) | 167-169

About the Author | 171

Acknowledgments

In addition to my family and friends who helped me through the most challenging days of my bereavement, I would like to thank the following for their help in making this book possible.

I thank Connie Anderson and Ann Aubitz for helping me wallow through the publishing process, and especially, for their wealth of knowledge and willingness to share it.

I'd like to express my appreciation to Connie Anderson for her editing skills and Marla Erickson for offering her gratuitous proofreading expertise. Also, a thank you to my sisters, Jeanne Anderson, Kathy Grafft, Theresa Nyberg, and Jennifer Kuzma, and my friend, Kathe Ostrom, who acted as my "beta" readers.

As always, a special thank you to my son, Danny Deveny, who allows me to embarrass him in my books.

Chapter 1

My Transformation

I used to see God in the clouds. Those were the days of innocence and pain. It seemed as if the pain made me humble, and with the humility I became innocent, almost childlike.

I started seeing God in the clouds after I died and was reincarnated—or, at least, that's what it felt like. God had, metaphorically, grabbed me from earth, blindfolded me, spun me around like a top, and then violently cast me back to the ground. Like a newly born calf I struggled to stand and tried to brush the darkness from myself.

Throughout my journey of being reborn, I put one foot in front of the other, fumbling with uncertainty. Then a commanding hand unbound my blindfold of denial, which had previously blocked my sight, and I cautiously took in the unfamiliar surroundings—a new world, a new person. Unlike someone with amnesia, I knew my name and my past, but like an amnesiac, my identity had been lost.

During those first few months, I searched for God in the

clouds. While sitting on my lakeside deck, the cosmic wisps of moisture would hover over my little world and morph into majestic shapes. I would gaze at their serrated silhouettes until I was a part of them and the magnificence they portrayed. And I knew without a doubt that's where I would find Billy, Dick and God. It felt as if my trio of elusive beings were sending a message through the clouds' conversion of changing hues.

Sometimes while I contemplated the magic of a cloud's massive size, I would light a candle on the patio table in remembrance or reflectively scan the pages of an old photo album—which would inevitably bring tears. But I had learned from my four-year-old son eleven years before, even though memories are painful, the release of tears is necessary.

Some of these things I did some of the time. But I never excluded one ritual while in my own private moment with my child, my husband, God...and Josh Groban.

Yes, Josh spoke to me back then. While my iPod spewed its music from the speaker strategically stationed on the deck railing, his voice projected around me, over the water, and rode upon the cool air of the night. And I couldn't help but sing along. My obvious favorite was *To Where You Are*, a song in which Josh is singing to his deceased loved one, but I also tried my vocals on others.

"*Un Amore Per Sempre...*" I would sing out loud, not knowing the definition of the words or whether the language was in Italian or French. However, I ultimately felt that it was my dead husband, and not Josh, who was speaking to me through those words—even though, in life, my husband could never carry a tune. Being the sole diva and director in my own personal operetta, I would unintentionally emote a bit too brazenly, never considering that the neighbors would get an earful. Even though I had an expansive view of the bay from my deck, our houses were but a stone's throw from each other. I had no reason to alarm them about the status of my sanity or lack thereof, but I didn't think of that back then, because my mind was only focused on the clouds.

While singing along with Josh, I would search the vast panorama of the sky for a message from my trio of spirits. I would sip from my wine glass until a message would come through the shape of a cloud or the words that Josh sang. The love would trickle to my heart like the warmth of the wine down my throat. (Yes, most widows I know *love their wine.*)

At times, I would look at myself from a distance, viewing a tragic figure, even though I knew by then that someone always had a more wretched story than mine. Other times, I would merely contemplate the sunset's reflection over the water, which would make me feel insignificant. But, I also carried a sensation of immortality. You see, I felt superior to death and the fear of it, because the pain was so intense. It seemed as if nothing could hurt me more deeply. In that moment, I had knowledge of everything on the earth and in the skies, because I could see God in the clouds—or maybe that was the wine talking.

Chapter 2

Labor Day and Chicken Noodle Soup:
September 2002

The moment I walked through the door of our home, the rank odor consumed me, and the humidity sucked the air from my lungs. All the windows were shut, which was not unusual, but the lowered shades that darkened the house had never been closed before. Our home had always portrayed the vast panorama of the lake before it, but now the rooms were hidden from the water and the light outside their windows.

Even though it was Labor Day and most people were out on the lake enjoying themselves, I had opted to work. Being a flight attendant, the day had involved serving soda to the masses, and my feet were still aching from (as I would proclaim) walking to California and back. Normally, the weekends were my days off, but because we needed the extra funds for the monthly mortgage payment and I was upset with my husband, I chose to, literally and figuratively, "stew" away from home.

The week before, Dick had self-diagnosed himself online with folic acid anemia. Because the diagnosis didn't sound serious and he had canceled the doctor's appointment I made for him that Friday, I was more upset with him than worried. If he was going to avoid facing his illness, he could just try to cure himself. I had given up.

I carried in a bag full of remedies that Dick had requested that morning: chicken noodle soup, ibuprofen and refills of folic acid supplements. Obscured in the darkness of the room, he turned toward me and opened his eyes from his prone position on the coach. His face was hued in a sallow pallor, and his eyes drooped with fatigue.

"Danny just called...he and his friends are out on the boat and the engine won't start...he's in Carmen's Bay. I just don't think I have the energy to help him." His voice was raspy, and his words were slow and measured.

"We have to tow him in, Dick. You just drive Ed's boat. I'll do everything else." Ed was a close friend of Dick's, and his 32-foot Sea Ray was tied up at our dock. It must have been irritation, or maybe denial, that stopped me from feeling apprehension for my husband that day. At that moment, I was only focused on Danny's dilemma.

Without concern, I methodically laid down the bag of goods in the kitchen and moved to the sliding door to let in some air. But even with it opened, I couldn't shake the foul smell of death.

Chapter 3

Vacations, Coffee Mugs, and Cheap Jewelry

While driving to the hospital on Tuesday, Dick sat next to me clutching his lab reports, unable to keep his hand and the papers from shaking. My husband had progressively become fragile since the day before, and even he could not deny that something was seriously wrong. The tests from the clinic that morning implied a blood abnormality, proving that the folic acid supplements had been a waste of time.

Glancing briefly at his silhouette, I noticed that his eyes struggled to remain open. He had on his favorite plaid shirt, although, it was not a favorite of mine by any stretch. In that moment, I reflected on how I would snatch it from the laundry basket some day and discard it without his knowledge—which would not be an easy task because he did most of the laundry chores. It's odd how we focus on the unimportant at times when we want to escape reality.

As my thoughts moved to the present, the visual of those lab reports in his hand woke me from my denial, and a knot in my throat projected into one lone tear trailing down my cheek. I blinked hard to stop a flow from ensuing.

"I wasn't very nice to you this summer, Dick...I'm so sorry," I confessed, remembering our little spats and my impatience. I should have given my cranky husband some consideration; after all, he was dying of leukemia. Although this fact had not been known to us that summer, and we were still entirely clueless to Dick's ailment while driving to the hospital that early September morning. I reached my hand toward him, and he took it in his as he spoke.

"No regrets...I want you to have no regrets," he softly avowed. By whispering those words, my husband gave me a crucial, parting gift. Because of this, I look back on the year of 2002 without remorse.

My mother-in-law died that spring, thankfully, she didn't live to see her son's subsequent death. Helen was missed by all, but she had been 85 with health issues, so her death had been predictable. When Dick started complaining about fatigue that July, neither of us was concerned. While my husband attributed it to his age—our older son, Danny, often teased him of being five months shy of AARP qualification—I believed his lack of energy was due to bereavement from his mother's passing. But despite my husband's weakness, he resolutely planned our annual tradition, a family road trip in early August.

Even though I was a flight attendant and flying was cheaper than filling our SUV with gasoline, Dick always insisted on driving and often got his way because he was stubborn. You see, my husband liked to "be in control" of his travel plans. In other words, he didn't like waiting in lines, flying standby, or sitting next to a sleeveless, sweaty man displaying his armpit hair.

Every summer "after Billy," our family of three packed up the SUV and traveled over mountains and valleys across the U.S.A.—we always referenced our timeline as "before" or "after Billy." I guess it was a good vantage point because we had become a different family since then, and we would never forget that date.

Dick was usually a procrastinator, while I could be described as a *pre*-crastinator to a fault. But these vacations must have been very important to him, for he would proactively reserve our rooms weeks before our travels. Because our finances were limited, we would stay at the cheapest lodgings, inns and wayside rests. However, Dick would say they were *quaint* lodgings, even though sometimes the toilets would not flush or the air conditioning was merely our ability to open a window. We would also forego the expensive antique stores and, instead, frequent the tacky souvenir shops where the shelves were lined with dust.

While rummaging through the cheap gadgets in these stores, I would often buy a discounted ring or bracelet, which would corrode by the time we returned home, and a Christmas tree ornament themed with the summer's destination. In turn, Danny would choose a flimsy, plastic weapon of some sort, and Dick would always buy a coffee mug with the name of our destination on its side.

My bling's destiny would most often end up in costume-jewelry heaven (the dumpster), and Danny's weapon would soon be buried and forgotten beneath his other munitions in his arsenal bin. But Dick's coffee mug collection continued to multiply in our bursting kitchen cabinet. It was a mystery about what dusty ceramics lurked in the back row of that ghost town of drinking implements on the top shelf in the kitchen. You see, Dick would routinely use his favorite and rewash it in the sink because our dishwasher had been broken for years. (And cleaning cabinets, or anything for that matter, was not my strong suit.)

Due to our monetary restrictions that summer of 2002, we set our vacation sights on complementary lodging at my sister and brother-in-law's cabin, as they would call it. Jeanne and Dave's lake home, which better describes it, was located on Island Lake, a small rural lake near the city of Duluth and the shores of Lake Superior. This was a much shorter road trip than we were accustomed to, which pleased me and disappointed our chauffeur.

We held to our shopping traditions that August and I brought home a tacky ankle bracelet inscribed with a *Grand Marais* and a tree ornament with Santa and his squirrel elves—reminding me of the squirrels we befriended on the top deck of my sister's lake home. After feeding them scraps from Danny's bag of Cheetos, these initially adorable little creatures mutated into aggressive, frightening rodents. Yes, lesson learned. Danny chose a slingshot for his vacation memorabilia, and Dick purchased his usual coffee mug.

However, I was pleasantly surprised that year when my husband bought a matching souvenir cup for me. Instead of our vacation destination, *Grand Marais*, each travel mug had the picture of a loon on its side. Well, I was flattered but didn't read too deeply into his considerate gift. I merely attributed his thoughtfulness to maturity as he neared AARP qualification—or possibly the souvenir shop had a two-for-one sale.

Three weeks after our return from vacation, while our coffee mugs were still adorned with the stubborn PLU stickers, I found myself in that familiar emergency room again and was soon to realize the significance of those mugs and the loon printed on their sides.

Chapter 4

A Grief Remembered and Four-Year-Old Wisdom

Our eighteen-month-old son, Billy, drowned on July 13, 1991—a pivotal moment in another transformation. On that bright July afternoon, I had sat in the ICU alone with my dying child in my arms.

Being 36, I had never experienced deep loss, the death of my grandparents hadn't even come close. Before my son's death, I had symbolically equated bereavement with a fall into a deep pit of despair. Then gradually over time, I believed, a person would crawl her way out of that hole and "feel all better" after, say, a year. I had been so misguided.

My grief was not one steady uphill climb, but better described as a roller coaster with my emotions setting the rails. The way I handled that roller coaster was to jump on and take the ride. Therefore, up and down, I rode the rails of anger, depression, denial, and guilt. It was truly a very nauseating experience. I was afraid that if I didn't confront my loss directly or, to put it in airline terms, if I didn't navigate straight through the middle of the turbulence, I would be stuck in a holding pattern circling the pain for life. And try as I may, I was unable to hide my bereavement from my son Danny, who was not quite four at the time.

One day, very shortly after Billy ventured into the water, I was in my usual spot on the sofa, clutching my younger son's blanket and displaying my typical torrential assault of brine and blubber. With my buttocks perfectly molded into the concave of the cushion, I noticed Danny at my side with anxious blue eyes gaping at the creature who had once been his mother. I realized, in that moment, that my son's greatest concern was that his mother, who had been strangely altered, would never be the same as before. I dropped the blanket and took Danny into my arms.

"Honey..." I whispered as I stroked his hair and gazed into his frightened eyes. "No matter how hard I cry, I will always be strong enough to take care of you. I will *always* be strong enough to take care of you," I repeated for emphasis. When his eyes softened and his lips turned into a slight grin, I could almost envision his impressionable brain absorbing my statement like a sponge in water.

"Okay, Mommy." And with that, Danny hopped off my lap with a levity that I had not witnessed since the day that Billy had left. It was as if he had reached out with both hands, snatched my promise and tightly held on to each word—but interspersed them in a way.

The next day when I, once again, succumbed to a deluge of hysterical tears while sitting in the imprint of the sofa cushion, Danny quietly approached me. He shimmied up the couch to sit next to me and placed his face in front of mine. While stroking my hair with his pudgy three-year-old fingers and trying to find his mother through the tears in my eyes, he spoke:

"Crying makes you strong, Mommy," he stalwartly avowed.

Crying makes you strong...From the mouths of babes, I thought and took my son into my arms and gave him a tight hug. *Yes*, I thought, *Danny is going to be all right*. From then on, my son and I held onto that aptly rephrased sentiment. However, my husband handled his grief quite differently.

Dick discovered that if he spoke of Billy in public, unmanly tears would soon follow. When coming home from work, he would find me sitting in the imprint of the sofa cushion, clutching Billy's blanket and consistently sighing. Consequently, Dick started to avoid our sullen home and ventured to loud, crowded places where there was no mention of Billy's name.

It felt as if we were both on that same roller coaster but riding in different cars. When he was on the high rail, I was on the low and vice versa—our cars would often cross paths but rarely met in the middle. We were in two different worlds, two levels of existence, two dimensions. It was as if we were drowning in deep water: treading side by side, trying to keep our heads above the waves, afraid to reach out for fear of pulling the other under.

Even though it was a most devastating phase of my life, it was also a time of angelic communications and another era of seeing God in the clouds. I guess when we find ourselves flat on the ground, maybe there's something we're supposed to find there.

But that's another story in the chronicles of the literary world which has already been told.

Chapter 5

The Hospital—Wednesday

"I'm not ready to die."

Dick said this to me the day before his death. His eyes were wide with disbelief, darkly recessed within the pallid skin of his face. I leaned forward to comfort him and he met me halfway, but the tubes were in the way of our embrace.

Even though the doctor had just told him that he had an 80 percent chance of full recovery, that was 20 percent shy of what he believed a few moments before. I assured my husband that those statistics were for everyone—the old, the unhealthy, the obese. Dick was young, fit, and healthy in every other way, except for the leukemia. I knew nothing about the word, but it absolutely scared me. And I had learned, by that time, that reality could sometimes be more frightening than the unknown.

When we arrived at the hospital that Tuesday and the orderly wheeled Dick into the fourth-floor Oncology Unit, we looked at each other with disbelief. He was being transported into the same room where his mother had died in four months earlier.

The nurses were also surprised to see Dick in his diminished capacity and greeted him as an old friend, or boyfriend. You see, I'm sure my husband had innocently flirted and charmed each one during his visits with his mother for the two months she had resided there.

"Do you want to be reassigned a new room, Dick?" the attractive nurse crooned.

"No, maybe this was meant to be, Carol. I can almost feel her here." My husband spoke to the nurse on a first-name basis and looked around the room, seeming to be searching for something.

After hearing about Dick's hospitalization, my sister, Kathy, offered to visit and oversee his treatment. This sister, of my four, is like that: a micromanager and doubter of the health system. In her defense, she was an oncology and ICU RN and had reason for her skepticism. But due to my husband's pride, he refused visitors until he was *presentable,* and due to his stubbornness, he was going to find a cure himself.

Being technologically ahead of his time, Dick requested that I bring his laptop to the hospital. But because it was 2002, Wi-Fi was not prevalent and a landline was not available in his hospital room. Furthermore, when he asked me to research his newly discovered disease on our desktop at home, I censored most of the dire predictions, leaving Dick with one paragraph of the only positive information I could find. Considering my hesitancy to face facts and his inability to get online, he agreed to Kathy's visit a day too late.

Chapter 6

Romeo, Romeo,
Wherefore Art Thou...Dick?

There's really nothing funny about a husband dying. Well, at least not for most widows. Although I suspect the infamous Roxy Hart, the Black Widow serial killers, and other lesser-publicized widows have been pleased by, or planned, their husbands' demise. Not so for me. In my defense and to my relief, the doctor assured me that I did not cause my husband's leukemia by spraying the house for cat fleas a few weeks before his diagnosis.

Even so, I never divulged this information to the life insurance company. It already appeared incriminating enough that I bought the policy for Dick only nine months before his sudden death. But that was the only lucky thing that has ever happened to me, if one would consider the whole circumstance as luck. Ultimately, the measly insurance money merely covered my time off from work after the funeral. Had I planned to oust my husband, I would have been a little more forward thinking and done the math.

Eighteen years and two months before my husband's death we had met on the shores of Lake Minnetonka, Minnesota. It was, and is, a self-proclaimed "party lake," and I will venture to say that we took advantage of its offerings.

From the start, I was somewhat attracted to Dick—tall, lean (almost too much so), with sexy blue eyes. But I also sensed that he was a playful, optimistic kind of guy. Although, that could have been accredited to our mutual interest in drinking alcohol with friends.

But, I could see through the platonic levity of our shared pastime that he was much more than most of the other men I had dated. Dick Deveny was ethical, intelligent and humble. When he walked into a room, friends and strangers alike immediately gravitated toward him. Of course, this was my first impression. And even though these traits were proven to be true over the course of our marriage, we were both soon to discover much deeper characteristics of each other—the good and bad.

After the first few weeks of getting acquainted, I asked my husband if I could call him Richard. He was quite offended; after all, his parents had given him the nickname Dick (bless their hearts). Here is its definition, according to the Merriam-Webster:

dick /**dik**/ *usually vulgar slang*
>   **noun**
>   > *a. Penis*
>   > *b. A mean, stupid, or annoying man*
>   > *c. Anything at all: "You don't know dick about this"*
>   **verb**

*a. Handle something inexpertly "Don't dick
around with the controls"*

In my defense, Richard *was* his legal birth name. Also, I
had a difficulty trying to imagine calling out his nickname in
the throes of passion. However, Dick it was and Dick it
stayed, and I eventually forgot all about its definition.

In hindsight, our three-year courtship was exciting and
turbulent, and our engagement was sudden and short, due to
those throes of passion. Mid-May engagement, early July
wedding, August honeymoon, baby in September.

Chapter 7

The Hospital—Thursday

My husband's last three days were chaotic at best. It turned out to be, one could say, a dark comedy of errors. Even though most of the infractions can honestly be attributed to the hospital's miscommunications, I personally overlooked some signs which could have changed the course of Dick's destiny.

In my defense, I was dreamingly medicated on Xanax soon after Dick was admitted to the hospital. Being I had never taken a sedative before, even a half dose was quite effective. Nevertheless, the drug was more helpful than harmful. A hysterical spouse is not a comfort to a dying husband.

After spending most of my time with Dick Tuesday through Thursday, I took a sabbatical from the hospital on Thursday night to placate my fourteen-year-old son with the good news that his dad was finally responding to a new set of platelets. While positively skewing the information for his ears, I explained that the doctor said his dad had an 80 percent chance of full recovery.

At the same time I was relaying Dick's prognosis to our son at home, back at the hospital the doctor was looking into Dick's pupils and logging into his medical records: "*Possible brain hemorrhage but not a surgical candidate.*" Then, I imagine, the doctor left the hospital to engage in a nice dinner at home with his family.

With this revelation, common sense would mandate that the spouse be notified and a CT scan ordered. What actually happened was that I, cluelessly, arrived at the hospital later that night to find Dick trying to speak in desperate, indecipherable groans. After bestowing him with a bedpan, glass of water and tissue and receiving a defeated eyeroll, I realized my attempts to read lips were inadequate.

Despite my Xanax-induced stupor, I did notice that Dick's right eyelid was drooping, but immediately attributed it to Dick's genetic lazy eye. But *because* of my Xanax-induced stupor, I forgot that it was his *left* and not his *right* eye that was genetically affected.

During the next few hours, my husband tried to get out of bed, pull off his oxygen and remove whatever tube and wire attached to him. With one hand, I tried to restrain him and with the other I kept ringing the call button for the nurse.

Even though vital sign alerts were relentlessly sounding in the hallway, the nurse on duty seldom responded. The bothered RN would appear occasionally to reattach Dick's equipment and exasperatedly repeat that Dick's erratic behavior was due to a reaction to the pain pills. This nurse was not the earlier-mentioned Carol. Carol would have devoted herself to my flirtatious husband.

While attempting to thwart Dick's attempts to detach medical devices, he continued to overpower me. We were in a painful, perpetual struggle until my husband abruptly sat up in bed and became motionless. His eyes were wide with discovery as he gaped past me at the left corner of the ceiling. With his arm outstretched, he extended a trembling finger as if pointing toward something very significant. I turned around to find nothing there, even though his eyes portrayed that something was very real to him. Did he finally find what he had been looking for in his mother's death room? I still wonder.

When his trance broke, he spoke in guttural tones and shifted his feet over the bed to stand. Feeling very alone and inadequate, I attempted to call my sister Kathy. Though several attempts were aborted by Dick grabbing the receiver from my hands, my sister's voice projected from the receiver above the deafening chimes. When Kathy found out what was transpiring, she instructed me to get the nurse on the phone "STAT."

Even from across the bed, I could clearly hear my sister's elevated voice as the nurse held the receiver at a distance from her ears. Like a souvenir bobble-head doll, her face turned pale and drawn as she repeatedly nodded to Kathy's directives. After the brief conversation, or should I say orders from my sister, a doctor was paged and a CT scan ordered.

To clarify and to make a long story shorter, I'll recap my husband's last three days.

The same batch of incompatible platelets were given to him on Tuesday and Wednesday, respectively. Because his body reacted with violent tremors each time, the treatments were stopped as soon as they were started. Then, when Dick's platelets were at an all-time low on Thursday, the doctor prescribed chemo—which I found out later, creates bleeds—therefore, an aneurysm.

Had my husband not been a stubborn man, had the hospital personnel been more astute, had I not been in a Xanax-altered state, or if computer technology had been more advanced, Dick may have lived. But that's regret and hindsight, and I promised my husband I would not go there.

Chapter 8

Confessions:
Not So Sweet

Another significant difference between the two major losses in my life was this: when my son died, I had to rediscover who *God* was—when my husband died, I needed to rediscover who *I* was. The world was new and so was I. My monikers changed from wife to widow, we to me, ours to mine, and I was consistently making room for a very large void. Feeling very diminished, I was only half of a whole.

But despite the daunting task of navigating through the pain and loss of spousal grief, I also felt an exciting anticipation of change. I tried to imagine myself a positively transformed person after being widowed at the age of forty-seven. Being faced with the challenge of self-invention, I had the opportunity to become more flawless, maybe even kinder. JoAnn Deveny could become that compassionate, soft-spoken, gentle lady who people describe in one phrase: "Oh, you'll love her—she's *so sweet.*"

Have you ever wondered what your one sentence is? That one sentence that turns on a lightbulb in the brain of the listener, and he or she immediately says, "Oh, her, yes. I know exactly who you're talking about!"

I wonder how people describe me now in one sentence? Definitely not sweet—giving at times, and practical most of the time. Yes, I could have become a sweet person after my transformation, but I blew it. However, I could blame it on my lengthy flight attendant career. Have you ever witnessed that vacant, cold stare in a flight attendant's eyes when she's anywhere near an airplane full of thirsty passengers?

My mother always claimed that I would have made a successful psychiatrist because of my vague, liberal arts psychology degree, listening skills, and, at times, placating my friends in need. But she was wrong, unless there is a new breed of tough-love psychiatry. Besides, she didn't often witness the new person I had become since my rebirth. I was usually on my best behavior with my mother.

Don't misunderstand me. I'm not a bad person. When my friends are at peace and without conflict, I'm the happiest. I've had enough drama in my life; no need to create it. But if I was a therapist and a patient came to me with a problem short of loss or illness, I would give her a glass of wine and tell her to buck up and volunteer at a soup kitchen.

You see, since my transformation, I don't take time to use a lot of pretty, descriptive words. When speaking, I tend to communicate in direct phrases. When others elaborate on details, I may finish their sentences to save us both time— very irritating and not good qualities for a therapist.

Particularly, small talk is not my preferred pastime, yet a major aspect of my job. Most days, I greet 300-plus strangers at the door of an airplane with the salutation, "Good morning (or afternoon). How are you?," while managing a genuine tone of voice and, sometimes, a forced smile. Then in response, they are socially required to answer, "Good, how are you?" And I must come back with a "Good!" "Great!" or some similar, positive one-liner. Why bother when we both know the answer? A more heartfelt salutation would be just "Good morning (or afternoon)," that is, if it genuinely is one.

Despite all my character flaws, I still have friends—or maybe they merely enjoy visiting my lake home, watching the sunset, and drinking my wine. Whatever the reason, God bless their comradery and deceived hearts.

Chapter 9

The Hospital—Friday

"Mrs. Deveny, you have to decide now! We have to intubate him, he's not getting enough oxygen..." the nurse implored while I paced back and forth, waiting for the results of the CT scan of my husband's brain. Even though the monitors were beeping, the IVs were gurgling, and medical staff were screaming directives at each other, I couldn't block out the voice of the insistent nurse at my side, trailing me like a duckling after its mother. After Dick's transfer to ICU, I found the new nurses very competent and *attentive*.

I've always said that there are more doctors on an airplane than in a hospital, and it turned out to be so true. Not one doctor was physically present at the hospital that morning, so the CT scan had to be faxed to a qualified physician at his home.

After the minutes seemed to feel like hours, the doctor eventually called the hospital and informed me that the scan showed a massive cranial bleed, complications of the leukemia and the chemo, he said. If we inserted or removed a tube, it would, most likely, cause Dick to bleed to death. Even if we succeeded without a bleed, my husband would "never be the same."

Hell, the day before, my husband had been worried about losing his moustache from chemo. How would he handle being mentally or physically disabled? So, I made the ultimate, life-altering decision for me, my son, and my husband. Dick, you'll be happy to know, I never regretted it.

The feeling of déjà vu overwhelmed me as I sat at my husband's bedside. The rapid movements of urgency, the monitors beeping, and the oxygen shushing through the tubes—all reminiscent of eleven years before. All very familiar, yet slightly different.

Even though my old friends of shock and disbelief were present, the rerun of my private horror movie varied in characters from the last time. I wasn't alone this time—my fourteen-year-old son was seated by my side. It wasn't a sunny afternoon as before, but an ebony night of torrential storms. Even so, Danny and I couldn't hear the wind and rain plummeting the outside walls of the hospital; only the beeps of the monitors, the rasping of my husband's lungs, and the sound of our own voices.

"It's okay, Dad. I love you. I'll be all right...You can go," Danny bravely avowed while trying to choke back his sobs. He held Dick's hand, knowing there was no chance of recovery or a normal life for his father. Even though the monitors showed little brain activity, Dick's fingers caressed his son's hand as Danny spoke.

At my insistence, the nurses were administering enough morphine to kill a horse. But, as stubborn as my husband was, he continued rasping for breath while his lungs filled with liquid.

Like Danny, I was repeating the same sentiment, because it was too grueling to watch both my husband and son suffer. And I imagined that Dick could hear us.

"It's okay to leave, dear. Danny and I will be okay. You can let go." But my inner voice was screaming. *Not again. Please, God, not again...*

Three hours later, in that early morning of September 6th, my husband died of a cranial bleed at the age of 49. Four days before he had been mowing the lawn. Three days before, he had been diagnosed with Acute Promyelocytic Leukemia. And the day before, he was given an 80 percent chance of full recovery. Somehow, his departure was too sudden for me to comprehend in that moment.

When my son and I shuffled out of that hospital that morning, I walked into the flooded parking lot and was blinded by the rising sun peeking through the vanishing storm clouds. As I climbed into the car, like eleven years before, I felt that familiar feeling of leaving something very important behind.

Several hours later, the glaring sun started to disappear behind the clouds into another black evening. While waiting for a sedative to kick in, I fitfully tossed within the sheets on one side of our expansive queen bed, and I was wearing and breathing in the essence of Dick's ugly, plaid shirt.

Chapter 10

Confessions:
Thou Shall Take His Name in Vain

No, there is nothing funny about a spouse dying—except for that one thing.

The inappropriate laughter would happen when meeting with a friend who lost her husband shortly after I did. "Lost." I never understood that term while describing death—I usually knew the location of my late husband, it wasn't as if I misplaced him. And why does one call a deceased husband "late"? Although, it was an appropriate designation for Dick because that's what he was most of the time.

This friend and my conversation always started out somber enough but ended up being more irreverently humorous than morose. While we reminisced and shared, an abrupt chuckle would regurgitate through our solemn words at the expense of our deceased husbands' names. It should have been predictable, because it was like that when they were alive as well.

Her name was Joan and mine JoAnn, but that wasn't the problem. You see, her husband was a Dick too—see what I mean? The two "Dicks" were very close friends. To keep them straight, we would always refer to them as "my Dick" or "your Dick," which often brought more chuckles. And on and on it went. We found it hard to carry on any serious conversation about our husbands without revealing a slight grin.

After being widowed, there seemed to be a necessity for moments of reprieve from the heaviness of grief. Therefore, sometimes a morbid-death thing would strike me in a peculiar way, and I would find it funny. You could say my behavior resembled a bipolar disorder—crying too loud one minute and laughing too loud the next. It must have been my mind's way of protecting itself from complete emancipation.

Having a spouse die is no reason to laugh, but there are some unexpected, ironic events that follow which break through the pain and bring some comic relief. Then, of course, the guilt automatically appears.

You might know what I'm referring to if you've experienced loss. You may identify with that shame that appears when you are enjoying life while your loved one's body lies in a grave. And when you start to emerge from your grief and feel a little better, not like the walking dead you were, the guilt settles in again. Guilt is a culprit that always says, "I could have done more," instead of stating, "Look at all I did." Guilt is a wasted emotion that will only drag you down and stop you from moving forward. Let go of it.

It's been said, "If it's worth crying over, it's worth laughing over." Well, not so much with death as other events. But, in hindsight, I've learned that you can't feel the beauty of a guttural laugh unless you have experienced its correlation.

Chapter 11

The Coffee Was Always Ready

When my eyelids opened the morning after Dick's death, like emerging parasites, the events of the previous day gradually permeated my thoughts. Dick was gone. Then the earth seemed to give away and my heart fell into a deep, dark place. You may have heard that adage, "Things will look better in the morning"—but not so much for the bereaved.

The first thing I noticed that morning, after reality punched me in the gut, was I couldn't smell that fresh-brewed aroma. Because Dick was an early riser—actually, just a bad sleeper—the coffee was always brewed by the time I awoke.

After a death, it's always about missing things. It's kind of like stepping over a hole where they once were. One less pair of shoes by the door, one fewer coffee mug in the sink, one less plate at the table...all missing.

The definition of a husband: The only one who loves your child as much as you do, who will listen without boredom as you speak at length about them, and who never tires of viewing their photos. He tows you out of snowbanks, knows everything about you and still likes you. He is the one you can direct your surliness at without losing his love, and you can flatulate or wear a facial mask while in his presence...or some of these things some of the time.

One would think that Dick and my experience with the sudden death of our child would have motivated us to preplan for our own burial plots. However, Billy's gravesite was donated by the Deveny family, and it was the last vacant spot in a plot of eight. Consequently, the last remaining gravesite was diminished by an oak tree's roots, and only a child could have been buried there. Seeming to be predestined, Billy's body rested between his great-grandma and great-aunt, both who had favored little boys in life.

Being my husband died on a Friday, it was necessary to pick out a burial plot before the funeral on Monday. Because Dick had been very much alive while mowing the lawn five days before, I was in denial and my decision-making skills were lacking that Saturday morning. Sensing that I needed assistance, my eldest sister, Jeanne, and her husband, Dave, promptly stepped in.

Like a commuter train with only two stops, they drove me back and forth between two locations, a Catholic and a community cemetery, until we were all a little carsick. Finally realizing that my mind wouldn't improve within that morning, I made the decision to bury Dick at the Mound Community Cemetery—because we had driven by it on the way to our baseball games, and it was located near water. Within my hazy thoughts, I concluded that Dick would like to be buried by lakeshore, although one would more accurately describe the body of water as a swamp, or "wetlands," by today's standards. And I didn't consider that

Dick had been a judicious altar boy, had attended Catholic schools all his life, and served as an usher for masses as an adult. My unsuitable choice for Dick's final resting place was another example why *my husband* may have regrets for dying before me without explicit instructions.

Before Dick's viewing at the funeral home, I asked his sister to help me pick out his eternal clothes, because she was a very detailed person and I was not. I almost felt worse for Diane at that time. That's what denial does, it makes you cast off your grief onto someone else, so you don't have to feel its entirety. If there weren't shock and disbelief, our healing would be much faster...but more unbearable.

However, condolences were appropriate for my sister-in-law. She had lost her nephew eleven years before, her 39-year-old sister five years before, her mother four months before, and now her 49-year-old brother. Even though Dick and Diane were often in disagreement, they still were tied by the blood of siblings. In the last few months before Dick's death, both had agreed to compromise while being the sole caregivers to their 93-year-old widowed father—who was her last family member remaining.

With Diane's help that morning, I chose an ensemble of business attire for my husband: starched white shirt, well-tailored suit, dress shoes and his favorite tie. Even though Dick wore casual clothes daily, he would never have attended a funeral wearing anything less than a proper suit. Well, he *was* an attendee in body—maybe/maybe not, in spirit.

While the lengthy viewing line stretched outside the door of the funeral home, the boys from Danny's football team came early and stationed themselves in the first few rows in front of the casket. Their jerseys were ink-pressed with the motto of that season: ***One for all and all for One.*** Even though the mission statement had been chosen a few months before, it happened to be appropriately supportive for the occasion.

Dick would not have predicted that his greatest achievement in life was his role as a youth coach. You see, when his car leasing business had faltered five years earlier, his self-esteem had been annihilated. He was a typical man of his generation who believed it was solely his duty to financially support his family. However, this turn of events freed up his time to coach Danny's teams, which ended up being his true legacy.

Besides the several boys he coached, his relatives, high school and college friends, business colleagues and drinking buddies attended. Even though I imagined Dick looking down with appreciation about the attendance at his funeral, I'm quite sure he wasn't pleased about the open casket.

My husband had never wanted a viewing. While I was aware of this, I also knew that many people needed closure because of the suddenness of his death. And Dick, my dear, the funeral isn't all about you. Of course, it was about Danny and me. I guess the lesson here is: don't die before your spouse, because he or she may do something you don't approve of, like write a few books about you.

On the way home from the viewing, Danny and I were chauffeured back to the house because everyone knows you should not let the newly bereaved drive...or let them near a loaded gun or a bottle of sedatives. While deep in thought, I vacantly stared out the window and suddenly realized that I had been anticipating sharing the events of the day with Dick. Once home, I guess I was going to tell my husband how he looked in the casket at his own funeral.

Guess what happened, Dick! You died, can you believe that! Evidently, that blindfold was still securely in place. It was easy to stay in denial, especially when his car was still in the garage, his voice was on the answering machine, his mail was delivered to the house, his clothes were in the closet and his underwear was still on the floor.

When I walked through the door to our house, I was surprised to see it empty, missing Dick. You could say I had not yet woke up to smell the coffee.

Chapter 12

A Stand-in Dad—and a Racoon

By today's standards, most people would say a family of six children is large. However, being raised in a small, rural town within the Catholic faith, the Kuzmas were considered more a norm than an anomaly. It was quite unusual—almost freakish—to run across an only child in Hibbing, Minnesota.

Within three years and two months of my parents' marriage in 1948, they produced three offspring. However, their spacing became more manageable after that first barrage of rug rats, and it took them a total of twenty years to complete their family.

While Tom, Jeanne, and Kathy were born at the beginning of the Baby Boomer era, four years later, my birthyear placed me in the middle of that productive period. Theresa arrived five years after me and became a member of the same club. However, Jennifer (oops!) was a wonderful surprise nine years later—born smack dab in the middle of Generation X.

Our parents raised children through: Little Richard and poodle skirts, Motown and mini-skirts, Woodstock and bell bottoms, Lionel Richie and leg warmers, Madonna and mood rings. But despite our age and generation differences, my siblings equally teamed to the rescue when one of us was in need.

On the day Dick died, my family, as only they knew how, swarmed to my house like bees returning to their hive. They had become very astute and studied students in Bereavement 101 and took up their roles utilizing each of their unique skill sets.

Some managed financial matters, funeral arrangements and obituaries. A few kept my focus on today and not what would come tomorrow. While at the same time, others prayed and kept my thoughts on the next world and a final reunion—quite confusing. My mother directed her daughters to attend to my emotional needs and made casseroles, while my father painted fences and patched screen doors.

After the storm that raged outside the hospital walls on that ill-fated night, the first week of September turned out to be the typically mild weather of Minnesota's early fall. Therefore, most of my consolers gathered on my deck facing the lake. Funny how I remember only a few details, but my contemplations are still vivid.

Several family members were on the deck with me the day after the funeral. Even though all the faces elude me, I remember that familiar sensation of standing still in time while the world was moving forward, and that nagging desire to stop it.

The conversation I most recall involved my brother asking permission to be Danny's "stand-in" dad. Of course, I accepted without fully comprehending the generosity and the commitment that meant for my brother. Nor, I imagine, did my assenting sister-in-law understand the duties that would be delegated to her at that time. After all, it's not easy being a stand-in dad's wife.

As my brother posed this generous offer, I noticed a large carcass washed up on the nearby lakeshore. It was the size of a young child, and with that, I pictured Billy's body moving with the waves' momentum. It reminded me, and all present, of another death...and the dark finality of it. As if taunting us, the lifeless body rocked back and forth, back and forth. Because time had no meaning, it seemed like it was hours, instead of the actual minutes it most likely was, that we all sat motionless and watched.

Because my brother was better at actions than words *and* a killer of animals, he broke our collective trance by rising from his seat and heading down to the beach to remove the rocking racoon from our vantage point.

The waves kept moving in and the boats continued to cruise through the channel. I could hear their passengers converse, yell, and sing in their drunken stupor. My young nieces and nephew ran and laughed through the yard, and my family spoke of returning to work the next day. But Dick was frozen in time. And there I was, stuck in the middle, between the living and the dead.

While time stood still on my deck, two women were walking on the sidewalk toward the bridge adjacent to my backyard. I imagine they were discussing their jobs, children, maybe even gossiping about a neighbor. Because they were a part of the living world, I'm sure they were oblivious to the static void only a few feet away.

Their trivial conversation must have taken a solemn turn when they noticed a middle-aged man standing at the far side of the bridge's railing. When the stranger suspiciously surveyed the area for witnesses, they may have even slowed their pace as they neared him. And I envision that they may have even gasped a bit when he raised a large black plastic bag weighted with rocks over the ledge and discarded its darkness into the deep water under the bridge.

Chapter 13

A Mute Teenager and Borrowed Tears

"Mom, I've decided to go cold turkey with my grief, just like Dad did with cigarettes," Danny proclaimed in the car on our way home from his dad's funeral. Despite my futile attempts to explain to him that grief doesn't work the same as quitting tobacco use, he continued to uphold his assertion, at least on the surface.

The worst thing about losing my husband was...sorry, Dick...*one* of the worst things about losing my husband was watching my son grieve.

After Dick's death, our home was a revolving door, spitting in and out an entourage of well-wishers. Because of this, Danny would often escape to the privacy of his bedroom for a reprieve. Often, in response, I would discretely follow him and listen through the door for the sounds of his grief.

With an ear pressed against the wood and the palm of my hand muffling my own whimpers, I would attempt to refrain from intruding. But most of the time, I failed and would impose. As I cradled my 14-year-old in his bed, he would embrace his dad's baseball hat and pour his tears upon it.

But the cries through the bedroom door were only apparent in the first few days after his father's death, and soon ended. However, this was not a relief to me. My greatest fear for Danny was that my son would stifle his grief, and it would erupt into unhealthy life choices. Again, I don't claim to be a psychologist, but I do have a good memory. You see, I had witnessed this phenomenon with my husband after our younger son's death.

Because I had helped Danny with his grief after his brother's death didn't mean that I knew how to help him after his father's. I learned that there was a significant difference between a four- and a fourteen-year-old's bereavement. However, I knew his unspeakable grief and tried to coerce it from him. But my fourteen-year-old refrained from talking about his dad and refused to see a counselor. Conversely, when Danny was four, he had so many questions about his brother's death, he would never shut up.

So with the limited knowledge from my vague liberal arts psychology degree, I utilized some amateur Freudian techniques.

Whenever a meal, an object, or event would bring back Dick's memory, I would verbally reminisce in Danny's presence. This discourse was like a monologue with no one listening. Yes, I was talking to myself, but widows do that. I discovered myself to be a great listener, never interrupting or disagreeing. That admission may also warrant a bipolar diagnosis.

After making a habit of this practice, Danny started taking notice and eventually would comment on my narrations. Even though he wasn't talking about his feelings (how many teenage males do that?), he was bringing his thoughts to the forefront and keeping them from becoming a pressurized cauldron of burning emotions. You see, I was speaking for him when he could not.

I would also cry in front of Danny when the feeling of loss moved me. At these times, Danny would silently wrap his strong, adolescent arms around me and tightly hold me until the tears stopped. To an outsider, it would appear as if he was consoling me, which he was. But I believe he was as comforted by my tears as I was by his hug. You see, I was crying for him when he could not.

His sturdy arms would firmly envelope my shoulders until my tears stopped, and even though he would never say a thing, I could hear that memorable four-year-old voice in my mind: *"Crying makes you strong, Mommy."*

So again, I confronted my grief straight on, as I only knew how, but this time was different. Having previously walked that grief path, I had a map and provisions. Knowing the road was rocky, I methodically put one foot in front of the other while I tripped, stumbled and fell. But I kept moving forward, because I knew, this time, there was a destination.

Chapter 14

Confessions:
The Regretful Closet

You can close the doors of a closet and believe that the contents stay the same, but ultimately their human smell is replaced with the wood's and the dust's aroma. If you keep those doors closed, you can imagine that their contents will be used again, worn in and worn out. But you can't pretend for long. Eventually, those doors need to be opened.

Because our home was miniscule, Dick kept his clothes in our bedroom closet and mine took second place in the spare bedroom. Had Dick reached AARP age, maybe he would have eventually seen the injustice in this. Consequently, Dick had his designated "do not trespass" areas, such as his closet, dresser, and tool bench. Of course, as his wife, I did not always adhere to those restrictions.

When I first opened the gateway to my husband's closet after his departure, the patterns, textures and smells affronted me. The shirts and pants on the hangers seemed to have an energy of their own because he had touched them and lived in them. They were not the inanimate objects they should have been and seemed to come alive like a spirit of yesterday's memories. They emitted a comforting aroma, a familiar ambience, and then a painful reminder. So at first, I waited unmoving, holding my breath, as if they would move or speak.

When I brought a shirt to my nose and inhaled the manly scent unique to my husband, a slideshow of images flashed through my mind: Places, conversations, hugs, and a life abruptly ended. I realized that I had taken those clothes for granted, assumed that they would always clothe my husband's body. After all, I thought I had years to touch them, speak to them—there had been no need to tell them how much they meant to me. They would never grow old or die.

It sounds odd, but the clothing that I had disliked the most was the hardest to discard, because those were the items that he preferred and had worn out. Ultimately, his ugly, plaid shirt became my favorite.

The most tattered items were his "lounging-at-home shirt," his "working-on-the-car shirt," his "mowing-the-lawn shoes." You may understand the sequence; my husband had a designated shirt and pair of shoes for every activity.

What surprised me most was that, my clothes held memories as well, especially the lingerie Dick had purchased for me. The fact was, I would not want to wear those items by myself—they didn't lend themselves to a comfortable sleep. And, of course, I would not want to wear them with another man. Still, I hung onto the sexy camies and panties, evidently waiting for my husband's return.

When I set to the task at hand, I first threw out Dick's underwear—that's it.

His clothes stayed in their allotted place for weeks until I found the motivation to make room in the closet and dresser drawers for my own. Within a few months, I managed to give up a few items that Dick rarely wore. After a few years, I boxed up the rest. And still, many years later, a few plastic bins holding the most sentimental items remain in my garage.

When questioned by others about my husband's possessions, my pathetic excuse is always Danny. I explain that I want to be rid of them because *I* have moved on, but Danny needs to go through his father's clothes when he is ready.

Truthfully, I also need more time with each shirt, shoe, short, swim suit and pant—to show them how much I appreciate them and their memories before I will let them go. So I hold on, as long as it takes to say goodbye—goodbye to them and their regretful closet.

Chapter 15

Spirits, Loons, and Roses

Dick wasn't as good as Billy at sending signs after his death. But I like to believe that, through God's approval and Billy's help, Dick was successful three weeks after his death.

It was late September, too late to be planting roses. My knees rested on the grass near the soon-to-be flowerbed as I dug the trowel into the black, dark soil. I had chosen the south side of the deck on the lakeside to plant a rose garden in Dick's memory, because it was a sunny location, and maybe I wouldn't forget to water it if it was close to the house.

This was my second amateur attempt at anything that resembled gardening (the first had been Billy's small daisy garden), so I was clueless but determined. The plants of choice were rose bushes, because Dick's gift to me for Mother's Day and Valentine's Day had always been four red roses to symbolize each member of my soon-to-be fragmented family.

After, and because of, Billy's death, I believed in after-death communications. I admit, had Billy not been so determined to connect with me, I still would have been cynical about the unseen. At the time I was digging my second garden, I had seen and felt things that could not be explained through reason or coincidence. However, it wasn't due to any innate psychic ability on my part. It was because God knew he had to whack me aside my stubborn head to keep me focused on life beyond here.

Contrarily, Dick had been a skeptic toward after-death communication up to his death. We had a few arguments on the subject, but to his defense, he didn't have the same experiences as me. That's why it was hard for me to imagine Dick as a specter, or as anything not grounded on earth, because he was so sensible—so black and white.

While the grass blades made an imprint in the skin of my knees and a brisk fall wind chilled my back, my thoughts spoke to my dead husband.

You're a spirit now, Dick...you probably don't believe in yourself. Because you're not tangible, does that mean I'll never hold you again? I miss your body, Dick. I need you to hold me.

A tear escaped from my eye, landing on the dirt before me. And then I heard the bird's call.

"Woo...woo" And again. "Woo...woo."

I looked over the water's horizon from where the sound came and scanned the lake for its source.

"Woo...woo." In the calm water near the end of our dock was a lone loon. While it relentlessly chanted, I remembered the coffee mugs Dick had bought a few weeks before.

Facing the water and the loon, my feet froze in place. My arms lost sensation and fell limp to my sides while the trowel fell from my hand. A light breeze caressed my face, and its warmth continued to embrace the skin of my arms, back and upper torso. My lips turned upward into an atypical grin.

"Hello, dear. Where have you been?" I said out loud and without forethought, for Dick, God and my neighbors to hear.

That was the first day the loon appeared at my lakeshore. I was amazed by this because loons were very scarce back in 2002 on Lake Minnetonka. But many summer days since, that lone loon...or some loon, at least, has appeared at the end of my dock. Even though the lifespan of a loon can be longer than twenty-five years, I admit it may be a different bird. And I sometimes doubt that Dick has truly mastered the art of clairvoyance. Nevertheless, I do know loons mate for life.

Despite the needed and healing disruption to my gardening that day, I managed to finish planting my four rose bushes. But when the next summer came, they were pathetic sticks with barely a rose bud apiece. Within two years, they died, so I replaced them with much heartier perennials.

But as the song goes, I never promised you a perfect marriage, a perfect life—or a rose garden, Dick; the thriving lilies and asters will have to do.

Chapter 16

Confessions:
A Fair-Weather Friend Named Denial

Even though I bore no guilt for Dick's death or how I treated him in life, I *was* guilty—guilty of harboring an irreverent sense of relief a few months after his death.

After all, I had no time for trips to the hospital or to nurse a sick husband while raising a teenager. And how would we have paid for the medical bills? Even though my thoughts were not as clear as all that, I remember feeling a liberation from duty. At times, I relished the release from an old routine and coddled the excitement of a new beginning. In between the chasms of mourning, I subconsciously took a reprieve and embraced the positive aspects of my husband's departure.

However, his clothes remained in the laundry basket, even though I would never wash them. I placed his mail on the table where he would find it, his voice still responded to our incoming calls on the answering machine, and his toothbrush sat next to mine on the sink. *My husband is dead.* I could say that repetitively out loud yet not entirely understand it.

It was soothing to wallow in my oblivion until I would open the garage door and realize that Dick's car was not going to move until I sold it. It all worked to my advantage, until I would be driving home from work, anticipating my return home, and then suddenly recall that he would not be there. Then the ground would give out, and I would fall into a deep, dark hole.

The denial was comforting to hold on to and essential for my sanity. But, really, I was just biding my time, waiting for my husband to walk through the front door again.

Chapter 17

Then There Were Two

After Billy's death, the feeling of wholeness was elusive as a family of three. One thing was always missing: a fourth plate, a fourth chair, a little bed, a car seat, a second hand to hold, a mischievous little spirit to love. In hindsight, I should have relished the crowd.

After Dick's death, the foreboding void was, once again, unnerving. It was as if Danny and I were continually stepping over a gaping hole to keep up with the moving world.

One must be very imaginative to pretend that two people make up a family, but I have been told that I'm a creative person. To make Danny and myself feel more complete, I established some new routines at home. This proved to be difficult at first, because I was unable to avoid overnight trips once returning to my flying job, until an angel with metal wings offered a solution.

This flight attendant was not a close friend at that time;

however, Linda proved to be so much more. Being that her seniority allowed her one-day trips and mine didn't, she traded her entire work schedule with me every month for the next four years, so I could wish Danny a good day in the morning and have a meal on the table before he returned home from school.

However, and as my close friends know, cooking has never been my strong suit. Even though I used my "galley kitchen" as an excuse, I just never enjoyed cutting stuff up and heating it. Another excuse for my lack of culinary skills were my picky eaters. When I cooked for Dick and Danny, it had been only on Sundays, and the main course was always roast beef with sides of mashed potatoes, gravy and an alternating choice of beans or corn. This was the menu choice every week for 15 years. That routine would even fizzle Martha Stewart's flame for cooking. On these Sunday nights, our family of three would place our plates on the coffee table in front of the TV. Heaven forbid that we interrupt our favorite show by praying or conversing. That had never been our ritual.

However, after Dick's death, I was determined to have a meal on the *table* for Danny every night. Being that his tastes were still the same as his father's, I found myself peeling potatoes and making gravy seven days a week. Yes, I was domestically challenged, but I eventually learned how to cook three different seasonless meats while still alternating the beans and corn. Danny was fed, and our family time was established.

Per our new routine, we set the table every night for two, despite the three chairs. I would say grace to God, Dick and Billy, and attempt to make conversation with my teenager. Even though we, or maybe just I found the new routine comforting, it transpired as you would imagine—like a talk show host interviewing an unresponsive guest.

Chapter 18

Friends and the Lonely Pariah

Friends are funny people. They're either with you or against you...or maybe it's just not that simple.

After Billy's death, I found our friends very helpful in the first few months, but then some gradually retreated into their own simpler lives. In their defense, Dick and I would have done the same had we not gone through our transformation. Before that monumental day in which Billy ran into the water, we were carefree, just like our friends. That's why I never blamed them for avoiding our solemn demeanor afterward. They just didn't know what to say.

It was the friends and acquaintances who stood at a distance, whispering indiscreetly while glancing in our direction, who I most wanted to educate. But I didn't have the energy or the words at that time. Now I do. For those of you who do not know what to say or what to do for a bereaved acquaintance, here you go:

- Hug them with permission. They miss the physical touch from their loved one. Talk about the deceased, share common memories. Also, share your memories that the bereaved is not aware of. In that way, a new aspect of the deceased becomes alive again.
- Don't be afraid of the tears. Tears wash the soul clean, they dissolve the lump in their throat momentarily—tears relieve the pressure. You see, it's a fallacy that you are bringing up their loss when you speak of their loved one. The pain is always there, hiding, like a predator ready to pounce when they least expect.
- Or don't speak at all. You don't need to fill the lapsed moments with empty words. Listen to them, their pain, their pleasant *and* horrible memories. In this way, you'll guide their way in silence with an open heart. You can't fix them, but your presence can cushion the sharp edges of their grief.
- Confirm their feelings. Don't judge. Don't rationalize.
- Don't say "How are you?," because they will just respond "Okay," when they're not. It's better to be more specific—"How did your morning go?" or "How was your evening?"—because the newly bereaved live one moment at a time.
- Don't ask how you can help, they don't know—just do something. Bring food, babysit, schedule a walk on a wooded path or by a reflective lake, where car engines, trains and planes are absent; where the silence is soothing.

One would think that, after going through my own losses, I would know exactly what to say to the grieving. On the contrary, I have tactlessly spewed many idiotic statements to the newly bereaved which were not helpful at all. But because of my experience, I know that it's not what you say or don't say that matters. They will forgive you, because you were the one who was there for them.

Just be there.

Chapter 19

Confessions:
Helicopters and a Football Mom

After my husband's car leasing business went bankrupt in 1997, he was struggling to start a consulting business from home, and I was flying as a "stew" four days a week (term only appropriate when used by flight attendants). This left Dick, for his last five years of life, as Danny's primary caretaker. Because Dick cooked his meals, cleaned the house, did his laundry, and coached his teams, their father-son bond had been very strongly established.

But despite the role reversal of those days, I would never allow Dick the title of *Mr. Mom* in my presence, any more than I would expect him to call me *Mrs. Dad* when I was alone with my son. I was a feminist of some sort, which is one of the reasons he said he married me. That, and my airline benefits.

Before his father's death, Danny had been a model son and student. After Dick died, I feared this would change. I wondered if Danny's only motivation was to please his dad, versus me, of course. Not knowing what direction my teenager would take after his father's death, I may have over-compensated a bit in the mothering department. Yes, I became a "helicopter mom," or worse, by today's standards, "a drone mom." And I hovered over every private moment of his life.

When Dick died we had just begun football season, and the day after the funeral Danny quarterbacked his team to a victory. He was, after all, going cold turkey. As a coach's wife, I had always known the inner politics of the youth teams that Dick had coached and Danny had participated in. While Danny and his dad discussed the plays, players and strategies of the game, I would quietly listen nearby and mentally take note to ask questions that weren't idiotic.

Suddenly, after Dick died, I was not privy to my son's teams. Not being in the inner circle of sport's politics anymore, I found that Danny was also at a disadvantage.

Some of the dads worked with their sons on batting, throwing a football or shooting hoops. At least, they knew how to break in or upgrade a baseball mitt. It was not uncommon to see the dads chumming up to the coaches, having a beer, rehashing the game—sometimes to further their sons' playing time. By observing, I tried to take a crash course in fathering an athlete, but ultimately, Danny was on his own.

Even though I was out of the testosterone loop, I was not out of the game. Using my only resource to the best of my ability, I made a lame attempt to flirt with one coach who happened to be single. Yes, I have some standards. Besides, it was all for Danny. It ended up backfiring on me after the coach discovered I was not even willing to take it to the level of a coffee date.

Because that strategy proved to have the opposite effect of what was intended, I arranged my flying schedule around Danny's games and practices to eavesdrop on the fathers' conversations in order to pick up any morsel of sports trivia. Eventually, I became frustrated with my limited knowledge, and as a defense mechanism, I became very proficient at bragging.

I knew, through Billy's death, that the future is not always a given. My subconscious rationale was that I needed to explain how talented my child was while he was still here. Nobody would believe me after he was gone, because the dead are always infallible. But that's another chapter.

Chapter 20

Where's That Brawny Guy
and His Allen Wrenches?

Soon after the funeral, one of my sisters called to my attention that I was a "widow." Sisters, you've got to love them. When she uttered that word, I couldn't keep a visual from entering my mind and suddenly felt an urge to run to the nearest mirror to see if I had grown a wart, gray hair, or humped back.

But a few months later, after acclimating myself to the title, I used it freely. The term and its consequences have formed me, but as they say, they don't define or reduce me. But, as I will explain later, there is a difference between a "rich widow" and just a "widow." So when appropriate, I would use that "widow card" to my advantage. In my defense, there are very few positive things about losing one's husband, and one must be inventive.

The first thing I did, at the suggestion of my family, was join the American Automobile Association (AAA, not AA), because I had no husband to call in case my aging car failed on the highway. It took only a few months to realize that *outdoor* lightbulbs on a house would eventually burn out, and the first thing to break was the toilet—and I was to learn that it would not be the last time.

I could only reason that a conspiracy among toilet inventors existed to keep the mechanics of a john archaic so that it must be adjusted every other month. After a few trips to the hardware store and a few chain repairs and flapper replacements, I remembered the male patrons at Dick's funeral and decided to play that widow card.

The women at the funeral had cried, prayed and empathized with me. But because men are much better at fixing toilets than feelings, their sentiments were quite different. I'm sure the men, who instinctively avowed to me, "Please call me if you need anything," really didn't expect a call. But, being the methodical person that I am and have remained since my transformation, I made a list of their names and their expertise.

First was Tom, the mechanical engineer. Then Rich, the car mechanic; Barry, the handyman; Randy, the electrician; Dan, the carpet man...and the list went on. In my defense, I used each kind person only once—except for accommodating and patient Tom, whom I bother to this day.

After I came to the bottom of my list, I retained Barry for my multipurpose handyman. Barry, who had co-coached with Dick, kindly worked for pennies and a glass of wine at the end of the day. And I always had pennies and wine on hand.

Historically being the frugal sort, I eventually learned how to find a wall stud, hook up TV to cable, check my tires' air pressure, repair a fence, run the snowblower, and change the furnace filter. But despite all my advances, I had yet to even come close to utilizing all the tools on Dick's tool bench. Yes, the tool bench was his; it would always be. Dick could repair, or should I say, "jerry-rig" most anything.

So it was not the kitchen, his favorite chair or the bedroom where I would feel his presence the most. When I opened the garage door, I could almost imagine a glowing aura surrounding the workbench and hear a celestial choir humming through the drawers of his tool kit, as if I were intruding on a spiritual shrine. Then I would envision Dick standing over his tools in his ugly plaid shirt.

It took me many months to feel single and even longer to realize that not only did I *have* to make all the decisions, but I *could* make all the decisions. Therefore, I moved Dick's clothes out of his closet, cleaned off his dresser, moved the furniture around in the living room, sold his car, bought a floral-patterned quilt for the bed, and got that second cat that I had always wanted, but he never did. But it took me a little longer to sell some of the tools on his workbench.

Had Dick been more proficient at after-death communication, I know he would have sent down a lightning bolt or some ominous sign after I traded his 17 Allen wrenches, metric socket wrenches, and a large metal doo-hickey for a couple bucks at a garage sale.

In my defense, the Allen wrenches looked like pieces of a broken lawn mower. And, I reasoned, if I didn't know the names, I didn't need them...only to find out later how much I did.

Eventually, I learned the names and the uses of all of Dick's *remaining* tools. Menards replaced Macy's as my favorite store, I was insulted if anyone offered to buy me a pink tool kit, and the chainsaw became my favorite electric tool. After an eighty-year-old willow tree fell on my house, Freddy Krueger had nothing on me.

Chapter 21

Confessions:
Booze and Embarrassment

Ten days after Dick's death and just in time for Danny's fifteenth birthday, the cell phone arrived in the mail. Dick had ordered it a few days before the revelation of his illness and perfectly timed its delivery by September 17th. It was, indeed, a gift given posthumously.

Despite my pathetic attempts to father an athlete that fall, Danny truly shined as a quarterback, making it the most exciting—and the most painful season ever. They were not bitter-sweet, but sweet-bitter moments.

After each one of Danny's lengthy touchdown passes (still bragging), I would become a spectacle by bouncing on the bleacher like a chimp in the wild and whistling at a decibel above the cheering fans to make sure everyone knew I was "the mom." Then I would turn to share my pride and happiness, but Dick wasn't there. Then I would taste that acrid lump in my throat and try, unsuccessfully, to hide the tears from a stand-in dad, his wife, my father, or one of my sisters who would usually be present. Sweet, then bitter, moment.

After one of Danny's Friday night football games in October, he didn't arrive home within the time limit of my comfort zone. So, of course, I jumped into my helicopter mode. While visualizing him bleeding in a dark alley after being attacked by terrorists, lying in a ditch after being hit by a car, or the victim of a falling meteorite (really, my thoughts would go there), I dialed his cell phone.

Initially, I was relieved to hear his voice, until a new scenario was added to my list of concerns...booze.

He was at his friend Josh's house, and even through the loud background music, I detected that his voice was slurred. Danny denied drinking, of course, as any teenager would, so I demanded to speak to Josh. While scolding my concerns and questions to my son's friend, our reception faltered. I hung up, threw my jacket over my time-worn flannel pajamas and headed out the door.

When I arrived at the house, Josh's parents' car was gone so I didn't bother to knock. Imagining that I would soon walk into a rerun of *Animal House*, I slammed the door behind me and stormed into the living room completely out of breath.

In retrospect, the ambience was quite peaceful. Josh, Danny and another friend, Joey, were lounging in recliners in front of the television, nursing their Gatorades and watching the varsity highlights. The three friends casually glanced up from their chairs with that adolescent vacancy, as if waiting for a light bulb to turn on. After a pregnant pause, Danny cocked his head with a smirk and spoke.

"Do you want me to walk a straight line for you?" he hoarsely croaked, and the other two unsuccessfully tried to stifle a chuckle. At least I was getting some response.

Even though I had been incredibly mistaken, I managed to stay in character. While trying not to look at their forced somber faces, I proclaimed with a demanding voice that, with Josh and Joey as witnesses, I owed Danny "a big one" — for lack of better words. Acting as if I had just chastised them, I sternly pivoted and left the room as quickly as I came, leaving behind my dignity and the boys' hushed chortles.

Eventually it came to light that Danny's muffled, slurred voice was the combination of his cheap cell phone reception and the hit he took to his larynx during the football game.

Despite my loss of dignity, I had learned a lesson from my knee-jerk reaction. That was the first and last time I accused Danny of boozing. However, it was not all in vain. That night, my son had witnessed the humiliation I could inflict on him if he drank alcohol or didn't inform me of his whereabouts.

Results: Danny never engaged in spirits while in high school, and I always received a phone call if he was tardy. So, ultimately, my pride was sacrificed for peace of mind. Whatever works.

Chapter 22

Wanted and Unwanted Dreams

I was across the street from him as he approached The Mist, our favorite restaurant. He was wearing the suit chosen for his funeral and smiling, making his eyes dance with that familiar playfulness. Like an old friend, all the feelings of companionship, love, belonging, completeness and security consumed me. Aching to touch him, I ran across the street while anticipating his familiar embrace. Because my legs seemed to be sluggish as if caught under a comforter, I painstakingly willed them a step at a time. He opened the door for the young lady at his side and turned to notice me for the first time.

"Dick, it's me! I missed you so much!" I cried out to him while moving closer. But when he turned his eyes toward me and focused on mine, they were dark. The familiar sparkle and warmth were gone from them, leaving a void of any feeling but utter disgust. The woman moved closer to him for protection. He moved his hand around her waist, like he used to do with me, shielding her from the crazy woman charging at them from across the street. They turned their backs toward me and disappeared through the restaurant door before I could reach them.

"Let me in, please...I miss you, Dick. Please!" I pounded on the locked door until I couldn't take the agony any longer. Then I awoke and felt the tears on my cheeks.

When I realized that Dick was merely dead and still loved me, I was oddly relieved. You could say that's the epitome of a selfish rationalization. But, despite the relief of my husband's faithfulness in death, a feeling of rejection lingered in the cobwebs of my mind throughout the day.

Since that life-changing morning of September 6th, I had prayed diligently for a dream from my husband. However, I was disappointed that I did not receive the dreams I had asked for. You know, the ones where your loved one holds you, tells you he loves you, misses you, and he is very happy, waiting for your miraculous reunion. Nope, never got one of those.

Consequently, all my dreams of Dick were filled with cheating and lying. In these scenarios, Dick had faked his death to elude me, he was repulsed and disgusted with me, and he was always with another woman. So, when I awoke in the morning, a profound feeling of rejection was over-whelming.

During those first couple tumultuous dating years, neither Dick nor I could claim that our relationship was exclusive. However, after our marriage, we had no reason to doubt our commitment or fidelity to each other. But still, the dreams haunted me after Dick's death.

Dreams are said to be merely a repetition of daily events or the closure of unfinished business. Or they can be repressed emotions trapped during the day, only to be released during the night when all barriers are down. All I can surmise with my amateur psychology degree is that, with the suddenness of Dick's death, I was left with subconscious feelings of abandonment and rejection. It reasons why these emotions would follow into my dreams; either that or I have low self-esteem. Also, Dick and I were immersed in denial and consumed with ensuing medical treatments during his last days, so we were not afforded affirmations of our mutual love or any semblance of a goodbye. We did not have any closure, and my abandonment dreams were not helping with that. Where were my closure dreams?

Even with my hypothesis and rationalization, the dreams have not entirely disappeared. I am a work-in-progress widow.

Chapter 23

Lava Lamps and Robbers

After accusing Danny of drinking, I decided to avoid any future embarrassment. So, I diligently plotted to lure his friends to my small abode. To accomplish that, in the 1300-square-foot, two-story home with no basement, I gave up my private living space.

The dining room table magically mutated into a poker table and the coffee table in the living room was replaced with a foosball table donated by my brother. My flower vases and figurines were boxed up to make room for adolescent paraphernalia such as an iPod, Xbox, drum set and a cherished lava lamp from the '70s. The refrigerator had little room for anything but frozen pizzas and sodas, and the cabinets were overflowing with pretzels and chips. In the winter, I would maintain an ice rink on the lake and a fire pit supplied with s'mores and hot cocoa for impromptu boot hockey games.

I admit that Dick would never have agreed to our only living area being morphed into a teen center. But, as they say, I built it and they came. Our home became a gathering place for many of Danny's comrades, even though a few would make a pilgrimage later in the evening to a house that offered something stronger than sodas.

When the first few boys would arrive, greetings were exchanged so they knew an adult was present. Then I would gather my snacks and beverage (sometimes a fermented one) and head to my upstairs bedroom where I could hear every word spoken through the heating vent on the floor. While lying prone with beverage and book in hand, I would catch up on the high school buzz and, also, monitor the gathering for alcohol consumption. Honestly, sometimes it was like listening to the audio book of *The Lord of the Flies* in fast motion. Pathetic—this was not what I envisioned for a single woman in her forties on a Saturday night.

Over time, friends of friends of Danny's would arrive to play iTunes, Xbox, foosball, poker, and eat my pizza. Some, whom I didn't know at all, were always welcomed with an open door. It should not have been a surprise when our house was robbed.

One night while Danny and I, apparently, were sound asleep, the crooks walked in our home and hauled off with our belongings. The police surmised, and common sense would suggest, that the perps were teenagers due to the list of stolen items: Xbox, iPod, drum set, lava lamp, and booze from the liquor cabinet. I'm a little embarrassed to say that a more mature robber would not be tempted by my worldly possessions. The greatest affront to me (besides the loss of my lava lamp), was that they used my own garbage can to transport the items.

After the intrusion, my father helped me install a padlock on the liquor cabinet, and I began to deadbolt the front door at night. Adolescents still came to eat my pizzas and drink my sodas, but my home was removed from the neighborhood teen "hit list."

Chapter 24

Chandeliers and a Church Lady

Even though Dick had often stated that he didn't want to be worth more dead than alive, I was more financially fortunate than some widows—the widows who were on welfare with several children, that is.

Because our friends knew of our monetary circumstances, Danny and I received generous cash gifts in memory of Dick in lieu of flowers. Also, some family members paid for many of the funeral expenses. Fortunately, I had the security of financial backup, which was a monumental relief. But I also knew that I would eventually need to fend for myself.

Soon after Dick's death, a dear widow friend tried to convince me that she was overwhelmed with household duties after her husband's recent death. Her list included calling Macy's to have a duvet delivered because she had tired of her old one (this is when I learned what a duvet was.) She also had the tedious task of deciding the destination of her next vacation to inform her travel agent in a timely manner. And besides those burdens, she had to make an appointment to have a chandelier installed—all this said with an exasperated breath. You see, she did the math and had quite an inheritance.

Some wealthy widows, who have large life insurance policies on their husbands, can quit their jobs, travel, and order chandeliers. Then there are not-so-wealthy widows—I ended up being the latter. No offense to those wealthy widows whose grief is just as painful, but I imagine I would have found a little more solace in going on vacation versus fixing the toilet after my husband's death. However, I did make many "trips" to the county courthouse.

After the death of a spouse, the barrage of paper work is incomprehensible, and, I imagine, even more daunting for the wealthy widows. Changes need to be made for social security, beneficiaries, house titles, life insurance and pensions—to name a few. And most of the organizations, who are holding hostage to our deserved monies, require death and marriage certificates. The county court house became my pilgrimage.

Soon after Dick's death, a few well-meaning friends often encouraged me to take time for myself, buy new clothes, or join a spa. In reality, I was a single mother of a teenager deeply involved in sports and a home-owner with a hefty mortgage and property taxes. In other words, I had neither the time or the money to pursue frivolous activities. Needless to say, I had to add an extra job and forego the spa. And when acquaintances would aspiringly emote about their dream list of vacation destinations or feats they wanted to experience before they died, I couldn't relate to their sentiments. You see, financially challenged widows are merely in "survivor mode;" we don't have "bucket lists."

But the biggest irritation after my husband died was when those people, who could order chandeliers, would say, "I'm so glad you're keeping busy!" *Keeping* is the problem word in that idiom. Had they left that one word out, I would not have been as annoyed. Or maybe just "You're so busy!" would have been more accurate and empathetic.

Soon after Dick died, the airline proposed a major pay cut. So, besides my job as a "stew," I subsidized my income by taking a job as a librarian at Danny's school for the legal minimum wage at the time, $5.25. This was advantageous for me, but not so much for Danny. I had access to the teacher's lounge and their discussions, enabling my helicopter mode.

Because my salaries were still inadequate for my hefty mortgage, I also returned to playing piano for church services. My college friends would have had an epiphany if they found out that the "Wild Woman" was a church lady and a librarian (monikers I never foresaw as a single woman in my forties.)

To clarify, the nickname my friends endowed me in academia had nothing to do with drugs, sex or rock and roll. They christened me the "Wild Woman" after witnessing my ability, and sometimes, inability, to hurdle tall parking meters on our trek from the pub to the dorm after the bars closed. At least, I mastered some skills during my five-year undergrad studies.

Chapter 25

Confessions:
The Apple Doesn't Fall Far from the Tree

I thought I was doing a decent job at the single-parenting thing until a few months after Dick's death. After years of ignoring that dark, dusty place under Danny's bed, one day an unusual urge motivated me to venture there. While doing so, I discovered a periodical of which I didn't approve.

The first thing I did was pray, some of it directed at God and some at Dick. So, in other words, it was one of my "why God" and "why Dick" moments. *Why, God, did I not clean under the bed three months ago when Dick was around? And, Why, Dick, aren't you here when I need you?* I guess they were not life-altering questions like, "Why are we here, God?" or "What's the meaning of life, God?" Nevertheless, they very important questions for me at that moment.

After Dick left me to raise a teenager, in fairness, I often entertained the thought that he was coaching a teenage boy in that Big Ballfield in the Sky. After all, Billy would "virtually" be a teenager by then. True or not, I liked to im-agine that scenario.

I didn't like confrontation any more than my son did, so I entertained the notion of taping a photo of my face over the centerfold's and then return the "reading" material to the exact location where I found it. That would get my point across without any uncomfortable discussions. After visualizing that situation, I ultimately dismissed that plan. No need to create a post-traumatic response regarding that area of his life. And I wanted grandkids someday.

After praying for guidance from Dick and God, I confronted Danny when he came home from football practice. As he walked in the door, I pounced like a hungry leopard hiding behind marsh grasses.

"Danny, I want to talk to you about something. Can you sit down with me for a moment?" *Oh, oh,* his face said. Usually, his dad was the narrator of uncomfortable soirees. The one thing that could have been a positive for him after his dad's death had just been denied.

"I was cleaning under your bed," I started, carefully choosing my words after we sat down across from each other in the family room. "...and I found something." Now his face said, *Oh, shit.* Then I took a different approach.

"Danny, your Dad was always a decent man in many ways..." *Dick was going to have to contribute to this discussion after all,* I thought. "...and one trait he had was being very respectful of women." *Good, good, now I know where I'm going.* "He treated his mother with honor, and he never bad mouthed me to his friends, even if he was angry." Danny was hanging his head, appearing to stare at his feet. "He always opened doors for women and taught you how to, as well. So..." *Almost done.* "...I want you to take that magazine out from under your bed and throw it into the trash where it belongs. And I want you to tell the friend who gave it to you, to never bring another one into this house again."

I looked at Danny. His head was still lowered, ashamed, I imagined. After a pregnant pause, he spoke.

"No one brought it into the house, Mom," he stated quietly. When he raised his head, I anticipated a humiliated countenance, but his face almost appeared as if he was holding back a grin.

"Dad gave it to me." He dropped his head. This time, it seemed, to hide his amusement.

"Okay...dinner's ready." I stood up, patted him on the back and walked away before I would have seen his body shake from stifling a chuckle. *Touché, Dick. Score one for you.*

The next day, I found Dick's stash of periodicals and disposed of them, along with some other paraphernalia that Dick and I shared which will remain undisclosed.

The paraphernalia was missed years later, but that's another chapter. And Dick's stash, being quite dated and dusty, could have been worth selling had I been thinking clearly. But then, those were the days of my innocence, when I was still seeing God in the clouds.

Chapter 26

Unanswered and Unasked Questions

After God disappeared from the clouds, I wasn't resentful of Him. I admit that when my son drowned on the shores of Lake Minnetonka eleven years earlier, my anger was raging. It was as if I was shaking one fist at God while desperately reaching for him with the other. But God and I had made amends.

After my husband's death, I started holding onto God with both hands, and to do that I had to let go of something. So, I let go of some defeating emotions. Emotions that I knew would only delay the healing: denial, anger, hopelessness—to name a few.

Those questions that hang in the air like a dense fog, the *whys* and *what ifs* that never find closure, had already been asked. Pondering these things again never crossed my mind, because I had learned from my son's death that those questions were a waste of my time and that they'll never be answered until I arrive in that place where Dick and Billy are. Be assured, I will have many questions needing answers once I get there.

Another experience lacking in my spousal versus my parental grief, I didn't feel intense guilt. Although I will note here that I was not a perfect wife by any means. But through the lessons of my previous bereavement, I had learned that guilt is another wasted emotion and defined only by hind-sight. I could only conclude that *guilt* is the act of condemning a previous decision *with* the knowledge of its consequence, and *living* means making a choice *without* having to know its result. So I chose to live.

And this time, I didn't blame God for the losses in my life. I came to believe that the trials in life are a domino effect from decisions and actions made by fallible humans, not by God or "the universe." I'm just not that important in the whole scheme of things. Nor did I blame Him for the person I became after He disappeared from the clouds. This left me with only one lame excuse for my character: my own stubbornness.

In my defense, I merely had the time and energy to go into survivor mode and stay there. How could I be considered sweet and innocent after that? How could I continue to look at the world through the eyes of a child when I had seen too much?

Chapter 27

Bah-Humbug

A few days after our wedding, I moved in with Dick (this was the usual sequence during that era: married, house, children. Now, it seems, the progression has reversed itself.) After living together, we soon found out how our holiday traditions differed.

In the Devenys' home, Easter baskets were hidden for a scavenger hunt, whereas the Kuzmas had routinely placed them in plain view to be discovered in the morning. My ideal Christmas tree was an apple and candy cane ornamented Fraser fir with white lights, while Dick preferred a tinseled Scotch pine with colored lights and hand-made ornaments from his childhood. Presents from Santa were not wrapped for the Devenys, while my family's Christmas morning enjoyment included violently ripping open the paper.

After much discussion, we agreed to wrap some presents and leave the rest in plain view. But because my husband was more stubborn than I, we had a tinseled Scotch pine with colored lights and a scavenger hunt was in effect for Easter morning. In that manner, our family traditions were established soon after our marriage, with patient surrender on my part.

Holidays reminded me most of the passing of time since Dick's death, and Christmas came too soon that year of 2002. Word to the not-so-wise: Do not send a newly bereaved widow a cheery Christmas card with pictures of a complete family on an annual vacation. Enough said.

The first year after a spouse's death, some widows feel more comfort in changing routines around the holidays. This can be done by moving locations for family gatherings, creating new traditions, or totally removing yourself from the season by taking a vacation to a sun destination. However, Danny and I felt more comfortable maintaining our traditions at home within the warm comfort of our extended family, while in the subzero elements of a Minnesota winter. (Remember, wealthy widow versus just widow.)

That Christmas, Danny and I managed to lift the ornament box from the top shelf in the garage without Dick's help. My son was aware of my shortcomings in the strength department by then and filled in for his dad wherever he could. With each vacation ornament unwrapped and placed on the Scotch pine tree, we silently reminisced about our summer driving excursions and mourned each one.

In this vein, we decorated the tree as Dick would have wanted. And even though I preferred not to sit through another rerun of *Christmas Vacation*, in Dick's honor, my son and I kept with tradition that yuletide season. However, some rituals were beyond our ability to maintain. For the first time in fifteen years, the Deveny house was secluded in the shadows of our street, lacking the outdoor Christmas lights which Dick had proudly displayed annually.

In the past, we would gather with the Devenys on Christmas Eve. Being that the Devenys were diminished down to Diane's distant Wisconsin family, we were included at my sister Jeanne's Christmas Eve celebration. Christmas Day remained at my brother Tom's house, however, neither "celebration" was traditional from Danny's and my viewpoint.

One could describe the gatherings as Christmas memorial services. On cue, the host families displayed pictures of Dick and Billy, lit candles, and said prayers in their favor. Our perceptive families were not afraid to freely mention Dick's name. Some would shed a tear and, at the same time, they were not uncomfortable with mine. Yes, they were professionals in grief etiquette.

When New Year's Eve ensued, I found my ear to the vent on the floor of my bedroom with champagne in hand. While listening to an adolescent poker game, I fell asleep before the kiss that would never happen at midnight.

Chapter 28

True Blue and New

Some astute couples, who knew that I would miss the routine Saturday night dates after Dick's death, continued to invite me to dinner as a third wheel. After being seated, it only took a few minutes for all to realize that vacant fourth chair was blatantly empty, and our relationships would never be the same as a threesome.

Nonetheless, our couple friends continued to invite me to their parties where the lack of one person wasn't as noticeable. Soon I found that my usual manner had to be altered in these mixed-gender situations. I learned that a *married* woman of their husband's friend was less of a threat than a *widowed* woman of their husband's *deceased* friend.

In the past, the couples would mingle separately, unaware and unconcerned about their spouse's whereabouts. But in my new position as "widow," it took only a few conversations with those husbands to realize that my socializing methods had to change. Within seconds of salutations with each of these men, his wife would suddenly appear at his side—placing her arms around his waist or clasping his hand as if claiming property. I can't imagine they thought I was a tempting catch or imminent threat. Maybe it was just a trust issue regarding their husbands.

Nevertheless, their reaction to my conversations with their husbands was quite different than in the past. Therefore, I learned how to address each wife, who magically materialized, using eye contact to include her in the conversation. This was becoming a learning curve for me. I started leaving the parties early—unlike the other women, I was lacking my designated driver—or not attending at all.

To my advantage, I was a church lady and a librarian, and my colleagues in these circles started including me in their events. But, to my disadvantage, these acquaintances were involved in libraries and churches. I found myself invited to more teas and religious concerts than lively galas. This was another learning curve for the "Wild Woman." Nevertheless, I forced myself to attend these modest events and never regretted it afterward. Later I found that these new friends (mostly the Catholics, like myself) also enjoyed spirited parties.

My circle of comrades eventually grew over time, mainly because I didn't reject those invitations. Ultimately, I procured an abundance of acquaintances who would put up with my terse, direct manner in exchange for a scenic sunset and a beverage on my deck. But that is another chapter.

Chapter 29

Holidays Will Kill You

When confronting the "first" holidays after a loss, I like to advise the newly bereaved to stay away from cold germs and toxic people, because their body and psyche are compromised.

I found that living through those special celebrations is all about *symbolism*. The experienced bereaved have been known to light a candle, cook a meal, visit a grave, release balloons or perform many other creative symbolic gestures, all to represent the memory or to incapably substitute for the presence of our deceased. However inadequate these intentions are, we usually receive comfort in knowing we are making some effort in our loved one's name. Sometimes we imagine that our beloved deceased is receiving the gesture with gratitude—and sometimes, it atones our unwarranted guilt.

With the arrival of January 2003, Dick's fiftieth birthday was upon us. In his memory, Danny and I bought roses for the cemetery-with-a-swamp-view. Afterward, we sat at our table for three reciting our usual grace to Dick, Billy and God. Because I was still domestically challenged, I bought a frozen Pepperidge Farm cake for the occasion and cooked Dick's favorite meal: seasonless roast beef, mashed potatoes and gravy.

"Well, at least Dad doesn't have to join AARP," Danny stated after we lit the candles and blew out their flame. *Yes*, I thought, *Danny will be okay*.

Billy's birthday came eight days later, so Danny and I brought daisies to his more distant burial plot in the heart of Minneapolis. That night I made Billy's favorite meal, mac and cheese, which was more within my culinary comfort zone.

When mid-February approached, the creeping dread returned. What does a widow do on Valentine's Day when the absence of her valentine is not fully comprehended? Even though this widow couldn't afford it, I bought myself a silver heart bracelet, wrapped it up, and signed it from my husband. Even though it sounds quite pathetic, it almost felt good when I ripped open the paper. Did I mention that I have a great imagination? Of course, I spent the day with the only man in my life and made Dick's favorite, seasonless roast beef, mashed potatoes and gravy. You may be noticing a pattern here.

By the time Easter arrived, we had established a routine but, because we celebrated with family, at least Danny could have some ham and cheesy potatoes.

On Mother's Day, Danny stepped up to the plate and bought us dinner at a nice restaurant—using the allowances I bestowed him—and we put daisies on Billy's grave. It was not a dreadful day, in retrospect; not like Father's Day, anyway.

That first Father's Day was most difficult. Losing a

husband, as a mother, means watching your child grieve. A mother's pain is magnified through her child's grief, a double whammy. Attempting to fill the void, Danny and I surrounded ourselves with family to celebrate the other fathers, including his stand-in dad. Three uncles, who were present, had also lost their fathers at an early age, and misery loves company—or, at least, misery finds solace in like company.

That evening, per tradition, we brought roses for Dick's cemetery-with-a-swamp-view and came home to cook...you know.

Chapter 30

Confessions:
First Dance and One Last Beer

It wasn't only the holidays that intensified the void of Dick's absence and marked the passing of time, but Danny's milestones had the same effect. A child's pivotal life events are the most cherished memories—and most meaningful when shared with a spouse.

I should have remembered that grief is an odd dance. It's a tango between denial and realization, a waltz with unfinished dreams and a monotonous two-step of daily challenges.

After the first year, I attempted to file my memories in the hidden recesses of my mind, as if they belonged to someone else. Because I was preoccupied with my three jobs, I did not heed my own advice on bereavement. I also should have remembered from an earlier transformation that if you pick an old scab, it will bleed more profusely than the initial wound. But I didn't and, as usual, I learned the hard way. To slow down, I had to hit a brick wall.

~~~~~~~~~~~~

"How do I tie this thing?" Danny entered the kitchen in his dad's suit, dress shirt and tie dangling around his neck in a square knot. Dick's suit was almost a perfect fit for him, except for the length, which I had crudely hemmed with masking tape. *Good enough for a tenth-grade dance*, I thought. It was February 2004, and my son was attending his first dance two days before Valentine's Day.

"You look so handsome, honey." As I surveyed my young adult in my husband's suit, visions of another life flashed through my mind—sweet-bitter snapshots of dinners, weddings, and New Year's Eve kisses. And suddenly Dick was standing before me. I shook my head to clear that image from my eyes and then backed away to analyze my son's appearance.

"Everything fits well...but...you need to find one of your dad's belts, hon. That completes the outfit..." and then one of those clichés spewed through my mouth without thinking: "Your dad would not have been caught dead in a proper suit without a belt." As soon as the adage left my mouth, I stopped, and a vision of Dick in his coffin came forward.

I can see how I forgot, but my astute sister-in-law—how could she have missed this? It was very uncharacteristic of her. We had forgotten Dick's belt for his final viewing, and I had just realized it a year and a half later. The irony of the adage hit me, and a smirk broke my contemplative grimace.

After making several attempts to devise something that didn't resemble a half-hitch knot for a boat rope, I sent Danny to our neighbors' house where a retired army colonel resided. He would know how to tie a meticulous tie, I reasoned.

While the husbands dropped off their teenagers and wives at the door of the hosting house for pre-dance pictures, I waited in the car line with the dads to deposit Danny and then searched for a rare parking space on the street a few blocks from the house. By the time I walked in the door, the women's groups were established.

I didn't know most of the wives attending, and the ones I did were interlocked into their private circles. Never having considered myself shy, uncharacteristically, I froze up and became a wallflower. While the wives were ordering their husbands to retrieve coolers and cameras, I was running a relay to the car, having forgotten mine. By the time I returned, the parents had dispersed, and the pictures had been taken. So, I took a quick photo of Danny and his random date, whom I hadn't met beforehand, told them to be safe and said my goodbyes. Then I proceeded to do the first thing that came to mind. I drove to the nearest bar to cry in a beer with some good company.

A widow and a divorcee, who had also seen their teenagers off to the dance, were my drinking companions. Even though they were appropriate comrades, I came to find out that they could both drink me under a table. Realizing my disadvantage, I said adieu to a full beer and my friends. At the time, I believed it was responsible to leave before my faculties were impaired, but in hindsight, I should have left two drinks on the table.

It turned out that if I would have just waited for one imbiber to leave the bar before me, the police would have followed them and not me out of that parking lot. For lack of any other infraction, the officers pulled me over for a dirty windshield. It was a bad stroke of luck that I had given Danny my clean car for his date, leaving me to drive his filthy one. However, I do not relieve myself of blame and do not accuse "the universe" for being against me. I just did something really stupid.

Looking back, I must admit, that night was not a total loss, and something positive could be derived from the traumatizing, humiliating experience. Ultimately, I (and my son) discovered the financial and emotional penalties of drinking while driving.

Most teenagers learn the hard way through their own mistakes. However, my kid learned his life lessons through his mother's. You could equate my life to an Aesop's Fable— there's always a moral attached.

Chapter 31

The Real Dick (Pardon the Pun)

*When a person loves you, not just plays with you, but really
loves you, you become REAL!*
(Paraphrased from *The Velveteen Rabbit*.)

A major part of my grief work was ruminating over the
missing fragments of my former life: saying "our" and "we," a
family of three, the third plate at the table, Saturday night
dates and a real father—not just a stand-in. I could choose to
hold onto those memories forever...but then, miss them
forever. These missing pieces, I learned from Billy's death,
are the secondary losses, almost as damaging and painful as
the primary loss. The primary loss, of course, was my
husband.

New acquaintances, people I met after Dick's departure,
would sometimes ask about him: What was he like, what
were his hobbies, what were my favorite memories of him?
When trying to describe him in a few words, I would find

myself spewing out his positive attributes.

I had focused on his favorable traits, because, of course, that's what I missed most, not his faults. Consequently, he became an impeccable idol. I had forgotten all else. Dick was ethical, handsome, fun-loving, exemplary youth coach, great father, wonderful husband...okay, maybe some of those things some of the time. However, he always had a full head of hair.

After many months of reminiscing about my perfect husband, one rainy day, I was inspired to rummage through the TV cabinet in search of old videos.

Even though Dick's image seemed to jump out of the screen, at the same time, I couldn't get close enough. I harbored a willful desire to reach inside the glass tube hoping to touch him. Dick was alive. Not just in animated, visual movements, but with audible sounds that aroused the familiar sensation of belonging to someone. Most of all, it was his voice that seemed to speak to me from the grave as if he had never left. My senses took in all of him, even his annoying aspects that used to drive me crazy. This person was not the Dick that I had been mourning. Ironically, I had been grieving for a stranger, not this real, fallible person whom I had loved so much.

The impact of viewing my husband in motion, not just a picture in a frame, made me realize the distance I had moved from him. A tear escaped down my cheek, and I remembered not only Dick's endearing irritations, but his frustrating faults. So I let the tears flow. Many tears had been shed in the past months, but none as productive as those real tears—remembering the real Dick.

I had recreated a new person in the past few years and, in doing so, had left my husband behind. Had I kept mourning a fictional character, Dick would have been lost forever.

Dick smiled at me from the TV screen, and I smiled back. *I remember you Dick; I'll never forget you now.*

Chapter 32

Pee Wee and Cathartic Cocktail Napkins

The characteristics of rural Minnesota proved to be inspirational—in the sense that there was not much happening except what you could conjure up in your own mind. Being raised in Hibbing, the heart of the remote, northern Minnesota Iron Range, lent itself to creativity.

As a child, I rode a small, dilapidated Schwinn bicycle named Pee Wee. However, for me to claim ownership would be misleading, because it had been purchased for my brother, the eldest in my family, and ridden by him and my two older sisters before me. I also understood, but tried not to dwell on the fact, that it would have to be surrendered to my younger sisters. Pee Wee's fenders had been dented and repainted so many times that it was a wonder how I could still balance, while riding with *no hands*, for blocks on end.

Many lazy summer days, I would jump on Pee Wee and make my usual pilgrimage to "The Dumps." This was the town's nickname for an expensive hill consisting of iron ore tailings (definition for city folk: Unusable residue and debris left from.the mining process.) Untouched and vacant for decades, "The Dumps" was overgrown with tall grasses and ancient trees.

Before making the trek, I would throw an old tablet of paper and a pen in Pee Wee's front basket and make certain that the baseball card was still attached by a clothespin to the spokes in order to create as much noise as possible. After scaling tiers of dirt trails and entering the vast forests of my refuge, I would shimmy up massive trees, build forts out of fallen limbs, or merely sit in the sand dune on its east side to write my first, and most likely last, science fiction novel.

The manuscript was titled, *Whimysphere,* but I will not bore you with its content, because it was never completed. After discovering *boys* in my transition from sixth to seventh grade, I abandoned my writings. And, consequently, its twenty handwritten pages were eventually lost in the chaos of a household that harbored six children. After that era, my motivation to write was mandated by a random English teacher or professor requesting a thesis.

However, twenty-four years later, my incentive to put my thoughts onto paper was renewed when my younger son drowned on the shores of Lake Minnetonka. That's when I learned that the act of journaling can be very cathartic for the grieving—putting the mind's ramblings in words releases and, at the same time, tames the demons of bereavement. Subsequently, my journal became the outline for my inspirational memoir.

At the time of my husband's death, I had completed *When Bluebirds Fly: Losing a Child, Living with Hope*, but had failed to find a publisher. The manuscript had grown to 400 pages, but I didn't have the funds to put it in print, and publishers would not take a chance on a rookie author.

Ultimately, I decided to prove myself to be a writer and book-marketer by writing a book I knew I could sell and afford to print. So, naturally, I wrote about my flight attendant career.

While navigating the airplane aisle with my beverage cart, tripping over purse straps, getting elbowed by oblivious passengers, being deafened by crying kids, I wrote down my frustrations on the only writing medium on hand—paper cocktail napkins. Within a few months, I had the equivalent of a Bounty warehouse of napkins in bulging manila folders at home.

While resourcing those scrawled notes, I designed my humorous air travel book and used what was left of Dick's life insurance to self-publish. However, the book became a means to an end. The book's success eventually found me a publisher for my inspirational memoir, and I expected that the profits would allow me to fly fewer hours—enabling me to hover over my teenager at home.

However, the leisure time I had anticipated was not to be. Between my flying, being an accompanist at church services, and my librarian job, I was actively involved in book signings, marketing and speaking engagements. (Yes, my chandelier-buying friends, I was *keeping* busy.) Amidst my hectic schedule, I often reflected on, and longed for, my carefree childhood at "The Dumps" with Pee Wee.

JoAnn Kuzma Deveny

Chapter 33

College and Meds for Moms

By the time Danny entered his sophomore year in high school, I started dreading the day he would leave me. Honestly, I would wake up at that bewitching hour of 3 a.m. and obsess about it.

Even though I occasionally socialized, the priority was to be available when my busy young adult came home. I didn't want to miss a moment of his life. This I had learned from Billy. Because I had perfected my helicopter mode by then, Danny's schedule was completely melded into mine, and his life became the whole of mine. My bedtime had gradually gotten earlier while Danny's had become later, so I would set my alarm to his curfew in the evening and sleep on the coach by the door to welcome him home and monitor his sobriety.

When Danny entered his junior year, he acquired his first serious girlfriend. One would think this would have motivated me to develop my own life; however, diligence became more important. For hot-blooded adolescents, an empty house is an alluring abode.

When it was time for ACTs, college visits and applications, I asked my doctor for another round of anti-anxiety meds. I hadn't taken any since Dick's death but was determined to make Danny's and my last year together memorable—in a good way. An anxious mother is neither an asset nor a pleasure to an eighteen-year-old boy.

Danny turned out to be an astute student, despite that he was not smart enough to leave his girlfriend in Minnesota. Instead of accepting a full ride at Notre Dame, he followed her to his second-choice college. If Dick had been around, he would have talked Danny out of this—actually, he would not have allowed it. But because I was not ready for Danny to be 500 miles away, and I still had football running through my veins, I didn't sway him either way. The college he chose was only an hour away, and he had been recruited to play football there.

"I put a binder in the top drawer of your dresser, dear. It has information on the nearest clinic, hospital, and pharmacy, a map of the school, bus schedule to the airport...I can always pick you up there...or you know, I'll come pick you up whenever you want to come home. And your class schedule is in the folder, your toiletries are unpacked in the top drawer of your dresser," I blathered on, while kneeling on the cement floor of his dorm room and making nurses' corners with his sheets around the steel frame of the miniature bed. As the chill of the tile floor permeated my knees, I made a mental note: *It's cold in this room, I'll have to talk to someone about that—maybe buy a rug.*

"Mom..." Trying to interrupt my prattle, Danny spoke quietly and somberly.

"...the laundry room is down the hall, and there are two cafeterias here..."

"Mom..." Now he rested his hand on my shoulder as he spoke. I turned my attention away from the cold steel bed and looked up at my son. Our eyes met, and his were full of love and concern.

"It's time to let go." That's all he had to say to rip a hole where my heart once was.

"Right now?" I questioned, still kneeling on the floor and looking up at my life and the death of it. Memories from the last eighteen years flashed through my mind as if our relationship was moments from dying. Danny nodded as he gently helped me up from the floor and put his arm around me.

"I'll walk you out."

That's how Danny left me. Thank God for my meds.

In those first few months, I continued to wake at 3 a.m. mourning the losses: no more skating rinks, no more eavesdropping on poker parties, and no more evening dinners. It took several months before I could pass by his empty room without crying. However, I was soon to realize that Danny was only an hour away, and even though I would miss our meals together, I did not miss mashing potatoes. During football season, I attended all his weekend games, and I continued shoveling a rink in the winter, just in case Danny would come home with his friends. By the time Christmas arrived, I was able to wean off the anti-anxiety meds.

As predicted by family and friends, the relationship with the girlfriend ended, and Danny reapplied to Notre Dame for his sophomore year. His essay the year before had been based on his father's life, death and lessons learned from him. That essay had won his approval into many selective colleges (still bragging.) However, his transfer student application for his sophomore year had to be better. After contemplating long and hard on how to top his first dissertation, Danny succeeded. The entirety of his second essay was based on how extremely dimwitted he was to pass up a full ride at Notre Dame—for a girlfriend and football.

To our surprise, the Irish accepted him again with full tuition paid. Catholics love confessions.

Chapter 34

Grow Old with Me, Please

As soon as my eyelids opened, the clock's light broke the darkness, showing 5:45 a.m. Time to get up. The house was quiet except for the chaffing of the cat's claws on my box spring.

Because I still habitually slept on the left side of the large queen bed, I had a clear view of the clock and Dick's picture on the dresser. I studied his face as I did most mornings. His hair was still full, his smile the same, and his lazy eye still slightly drooped and stared at me from the frame.

I reflected on how I had taken Dick's good looks for granted, until he became timeless in the picture on my dresser. Yes, it was my dresser now; everything was *just mine*. I had finally become accustomed to saying *my* instead of *our*.

While rolling out of bed and placing my feet on the floor, I was startled by the cat's screech.

"Sorry, sorry, sorry, Charlie!" I bent over to coddle my

feline, but still affronted, he recoiled and crawled under the bed. *He'll forgive me as soon as I run the can opener for his Friskies,* I thought.

At the bathroom sink, I grabbed my toothbrush and looked in the mirror to study my face. *When did I start looking like my mother?* While brushing my teeth, I stared in awe at a strange flap of skin waving at me from underneath my biceps. Foolishly, I proceeded to set down my toothbrush and grab the hand-held mirror on the counter. When turning my backside to the mirror, I discovered that my once-firm butt was starting to become one with my thighs and two nippleless breasts were forming below my scapula.

How old are you now, Dick? Are you remaining timeless like that picture on my dresser, and when we meet again you will be a young man and I, an elderly woman. Not an ideal scenario for either of us. Or will we be wisps of clouds or invisible souls with no bodies at all—with no physical means to touch, hug, or cuddle?

When you grow old with your spouse, you can stay in denial and remain young together in your own minds. I guess everything is relative—our view of the world is formed by our comparisons. When a wife grows old with her spouse, she doesn't focus on his wrinkles or saggy skin because the change is gradual. In a magical oblivion, she can still look through the eyes of youth, seeing him as she met him— unless she puts on her cheaters and concentrates on the flaws. And when his ears start getting too large for his head, she ignores them, because she is developing new breasts on her back.

But because the picture of my husband on my dresser was frozen in time, I was aging and leaving him behind in his youth. Our age difference was becoming apparent.

Damn. Time to join a gym, I thought. While discarding the mirror to the bathroom counter, I tried to erase the image of my backside from my mind.

Chapter 35

The Produce Guy, His Wife, and a Gun

At the time I discovered my underarms waving at me, statistics revealed that *widowers* usually remarry within a year after their spouse dies. However, *widows* marry after five years, or never. It had already been six years since Dick's death and I had surpassed that "never" verdict. I began to feel an urgency to find a companion before my back-breasts and butt got any bigger. However, my goal was not to find a husband, but the definition of one. You know, a person who really knows me well and still likes me. That scenario usually takes years—and I didn't have years.

You could say that time started to matter to me after I noticed Dick's picture was still 49 and my face wasn't anymore. But, even though my handheld mirror didn't lie, I still tended to remain in denial. The men my age looked ancient. Was I really that old? The answer, of course, was yes, despite my compelling desire to disable the hands of time.

During the first few years after Dick's death, except for harmless flirting with coaches, I never considered the thought of dating. A few men had asked me out, to no avail. My reality was that if I walked into a room, the shortest, baldest, heaviest man would approach me. And when I attended my 35th reunion that summer of 2008, some male classmates didn't recognize me, and not because I didn't make an impression on them in my teens. That year, when I discovered my underarms waving at me, Danny was away at college and I had turned 53. It was time to get serious.

It all started in the produce aisle of a local grocery store. Of course, it was the produce guy who asked me out, I would have never had the guts. He was 40 years-old, fancied older women, and, coincidently, had an uncanny resemblance to Josh Groban.

It was an innocent and enjoyable dating experience, until he wanted more...and I found out he was married *and* had a jealous ex-girlfriend who owned a gun. Honestly, I don't write fiction books; I couldn't make this up.

But, once again, the experience was not in vain, and a lesson was learned. Not only did I learn how to pick out a ripe cantaloupe and how to break asparagus spears, the experience motivated me to revisit the sensible routine of locking my front door at night.

Not to be deterred by my first dating experience, I kept my eyes open to other options. But I was soon to discover that I was inadequate in the philandering department; I didn't have a clue. After eighteen years of married life and trying not to lead men on, I had forgotten how to flirt. When attempting, I would, at first, freeze in mid-motion, not knowing what to do with my appendages hanging at my sides. Then I would morph into an anal-retentive Franciscan nun during a code of silence. As you would imagine, this was not an attractive first impression.

Because of my incompetence in conversing with men I was attracted to, I had to come to terms that I wasn't such a catch after all and, therefore, should lower my standards. Maybe I should settle for that short, heavy, bald guy?

...Nah.

Chapter 36

We're Not a Match

It wasn't only my aging appearance that motivated me to date; there was outside pressure from a certain family member. I thought my experience with the produce guy would stifle my brother's badgering, but he was relentless. Any discussion about broken toilets or college expenses brought up the subject of finding a man.

Despite my brother's lack of filters when speaking, he is a kind person. Nevertheless, his motives may not have been entirely about concern for my happiness but apprehension that he'd have to support me in my old age if I didn't find a wealthy suitor. To stop his persistent needling, and to broaden my selection outside the radius of rural Mound, Minnesota, I designed my profile on Match.com.

After much time and thought, I created a synopsis of myself for the website. My profile went something like this:

I am a 53-year-old widow, author, mother, accom-

panist, and flight attendant. I enjoy rollerblading, boating, running and relishing the beautiful sunsets from my lakeside deck. I am financially capable of supporting myself and my son, who is away at college, so I'm not looking for a hand-out. After my husband died, my love is dangling in midair, just waiting for someone to accept it...

Then, to add the finishing touch, I chose a blurry, complimentary profile picture that didn't depict the wrinkle lines around my eyes. In hindsight, it was not the best choice.

I was to learn that it's not good to look better in a Match profile picture than in real life. The moment I pushed the save button, every Match male, who had been stalking new members within a 60-mile radius of Minneapolis, started messaging me. Honestly, the first day there were over forty responses, then, thank goodness, they tapered off a bit afterward. While scanning the pictures and profiles on my computer screen, I couldn't help but feel like a victim reviewing a police lineup. It was overwhelming, and yet, a bit exciting.

I started responding to the messages. *Sorry, we're not a match, sorry we're not a match, sorry we're not a match.* However, I didn't feel the courtesy or need to respond to all. The boys in their twenties, who had crouch shots for profile pictures, and the older men, in dirty t-shirts, sporting unkempt beard growth, and clutching a beer as though it would run away, were just deleted. Ultimately, I was left with a 1-out-of-10 ratio of acceptable men. And that's how I eventually found my 38 first dates in one year.

In my youth, I had not been a stereotypical female who sought to find that one soul mate, but, rather, I explored my options to a fault. When I was looking for a good time, many of my female peers were looking for commitment and financial potential. Unfortunately, my mother never taught me the material side of marriage. But some mothers did, so those twenty-something daughters often wanted somebody to take care of them financially and emotionally and were actively searching for a spouse. But, typically, the young men in their twenties were running from all of that. Oddly enough, I found that the dating game had reinvented itself in a role reversal since my youth.

After finding myself single in my fifties, I found that it was the women running from commitment, and the men wanting a caretaker. In other words, the women had wised up with their maturity and the men had become needy. As the adage goes, the dear old boys wanted "a nurse and a purse."

And instead of bestowing their dates with bouquets of flowers, as in their youth, older men would gift tomatoes from their gardens. Which was fine by me; I always thought flowers were overrated.

Chapter 37

38 First Dates

For my first-first online date, we met at a coffee house at a central location for both of us. It was my suggestion, because the scenario would indicate that I wanted to take things slow, right?

While sipping coffee, I tried to keep my mind open while he led every conversation into a sexual theme. I thought it odd, but maybe that was normal dating conversation in the new millennium? When he ran out of wind, we departed the coffee house, and he walked me to my car. In the moment, I thought that was charming, but when he abruptly smacked me on the lips and ran to his car, I completely understood the phrase "stealing a kiss." He was out of the parking lot before I realized what had happened. My first-first date and my first kiss since Dick left. Not ideal. I scrubbed my face when I got home.

My second-first date was an invitation for breakfast. At first glance upon arrival, I wondered if the guy had sent a friend in his place. It was then I learned the first decree of Match.com: Nobody looks like their profile picture. Being that it would be awkward to turn around and walk out before sitting down, I introduced myself and ordered a water and fruit—that way I could make the date short and sweet, if needed. Realizing that was not going to be the case after he ordered an "everything omelet" with waffles, hash browns, bacon and coffee, I had no choice but to conjure up conversation. After a tedious hour of idle chatter, the bill finally came. Without humility, he handed the waitress a 50 percent off coupon and asked her to split the bill between us. Despite his thriftiness, I didn't find *anything* but his "*everything* omelet" attractive about him. I should have ordered one.

Despite my first few experiences, I was optimistic about my third-first date after studying his profile picture. He looked rather attractive; kneeling on his dock, wearing a plaid flannel shirt, baggy blue jeans, and a baseball cap with a lure hanging from the brim. I thought, maybe an outdoorsman could be my type, even though "my type" hadn't been narrowed down to any definition by that point. And he looked okay in his fishing gear, at the distance the photo was taken, he would look even better when he cleaned up, I imagined.

When entering the restaurant for our lunch date, I immediately recognized my date at a table on the establishment's deck. However, it wasn't his face that was recognizable, but his clothes. Yup, he was wearing the same plaid flannel shirt, baggy blue jeans, and baseball hat with the lure still hanging from its brim. It didn't take a genius to realize that he had a limited choice of wardrobe and not much fashion sense. Maybe he wasn't even a fisherman after all? Anyway, he ended up being an okay guy and a fine conversationalist, but he was a little too short and heavy for me. And after his cap blew off in the wind, I noticed, bald as well.

I may be coming across as very shallow with my criteria. It is undeniable many handsome men are bald, and "lookers" can be short or heavy. But I seem to not have chemistry for a man with all three traits.

Not to be discouraged, I embarked on my fourth-first date, and he turned out to be a physically attractive man. However, after he explained, with a straight face, why he divorced his wife and mother of his four children, he became ugly. You see, his bothersome wife of 20 years had to set the alarm for work and would inadvertently awake him early in the morning. And he was tired of it. One could appreciate his honesty, but he was, obviously, not a prime candidate for an unconditional relationship.

Halfway through my fifth-first date, I deliberately sabotaged any chance of a second. He was not bad looking, and I admit his face was as complementary in person as it was in his profile face photo. But what the picture didn't show was that his head kept growing after adolescence and his body did not. Once again, very superficial and catty, let's just say there was no chemistry between us.

I sipped my coffee while being mesmerized by my sixth-first date, or, should I say, by his ability to narrate bicycling stories without taking a breath between sentences. Not being an avid fan of serious road cycling, I bided my time with patience, eye contact, an occasional nod and "ah-ha." But when he started to complain about motorists, in my neck of the woods, honking and cursing at him while he felt entitled to hog the road, I found my out. But to get a word in brought me back to grade school—the timing was like trying to lunge into a rotating jump rope. When succeeding, I proclaimed that I was probably one of those motorists who had thrown profanities at him while he blocked the two-lane road with no shoulder and a listed speed limit of 55.

On record, that was my shortest first date. I quickly left the restaurant that day, while nodding adieu to the waitresses and the hostess. You see, most of my dates and I met at the same establishment, which was equidistant between my house in a western rural community and the rest of the world. Because the staff was a constant while my dates were not, I was fodder for their entertainment on a slow business day. During these dates, I had often caught restaurant staff scrutinizing me and my mismatched date while camouflaged behind the cash register or kitchen counter.

Observing my seventh-first date as he showed me to a table at my usual restaurant, I noted that this New Yorker was quite attractive. When arriving, I rounded the table to sit down, but he redirected me to a different chair which he had pulled out for me. At first, I thought this was pleasantly chivalrous, until I got to know him within a matter of seconds. Arrogant, obnoxious and critical, come to mind. After critiquing my wardrobe and correcting me on the most efficient way to shovel an ice rink, I realized he had positioned my face to the bright sunlight of the window, leaving no flaw or wrinkle undetected. How dare a man from New York City, who only viewed the Times Square ice rink from the distance of his penthouse, tell me how to shovel a rink?

Mister "pretend fisherman" with one set of clothes was starting to look good to me.

...Nah.

Chapter 38

Confessions:
Bravery and Brain Injuries

Because of my failure to find one "Match," I realized my profile needed alterations. It didn't necessarily need a new picture or more credentials, I just needed to be more specific. After a little time and thought, but much resolution, my new essay went something like this:

If your profile picture shows you on your Harley sporting a ponytail and tattoos, I'm probably not the match for you. I don't enjoy Piña Coladas or getting caught in the rain, but I do like a good glass of wine and someone to treat me to it. I can support myself but would like to be pampered for the first time in my life...you pay for the meal. Friends first, before physical, and I'd like to take it slow. I don't like to waste my time talking to you on the phone, emailing, or texting. Let's meet and get it over with. I prefer no calls, texting, calling during the week, just a lavish Saturday night date at a nice restaurant would be perfect.

Needless to say, I had few responses, but of the few, I met some very pleasant...short, bald, and heavy men. I eventually realized that online dating was not an efficient way for me to meet a companion. My scenario would have to be across a crowded room with that chemistry-thing involved.

So, after 38 first dates, I canceled my membership on Match.com. However, life is a series of lessons, and I don't regret my experience. After all, I became very apt at first dates but had no clue what to do on a second.

After a few months' sabbatical from dating, I started going through withdrawals from the excitement of the chase. One day, when having lunch with a gal pal at my oft-frequented restaurant, I decided to take matters into my own hands.

From my seat in the dining room, I spied a handsome guy at the restaurant bar. He had a soft drink in hand—not imbibing at noon. Good. Check. He was reading a newspaper—aware of current events and probably literate. Good. Check. His clothes were tasteful and clean—possibly had more than one outfit. Good. Check.

Being neither drunk nor brave, I slipped my card next to his soft drink before I dashed out of the restaurant without looking back. Only a few moments after racing out of the parking lot, he texted me.

I must admit that I was very hopeful and excited to see him on our first date. He had picked an expensive restaurant and sounded rather charming in his text messages before-hand. When we met, he looked as attractive as I remembered and pulled out a seat for me at the dimly lit bar. However, within a few moments, I realized something was a bit off.

Despite graduating from a selective college, his speech was a little slow as he weighed his every word. I suppose I could have excused his several cigarette breaks or his stammers. But when he started referring to every event as before or after "the accident," I realized a meaningful conversation was not in the cards.

I'm sure that the dating gods were somewhere messing with my head and laughing at my expense because of my shallow standards. Having finally found physical attraction, couldn't they have given me just one other positive attribute?

Maybe it was a little selfish to ignore his future calls and texts. But at my age, I knew I couldn't take care of a brain-damaged, cancer-ridden man *and* my college student.

Chapter 39

Blind Dates and Dick Van Dyke

Disillusioned and exhausted, I gave up looking for dates online...or at a bar, which always made me feel like the crazy stalker in *Play Misty for Me*. However, I was still open to being set up by acquaintances and friends. And that's when I learned why it is called a "blind date."

One such date *started* well. He was dressed fashionably and opened doors for me, but it soon went downhill. During appetizers, we argued about the "inadequate" youth football programs in my community—which my husband had started years before he died. During dinner, we disagreed on college choices, politics, and religion. And we continued to contradict each other all the way through the after-dinner coffee—not a good indication for the future.

Another blind date was very kind, intelligent, chivalrous and caring—but was almost three inches shorter than me, balding, and with very distinctive Norwegian features. Obviously, that friend didn't know my prejudices. Yes, my standards were set too high without merit.

Another friend must not have known my age and set me up with a man ten years my junior. I'll admit some people say I look younger than I am—in the right lighting, that is. But any man with the credentials I have set, and in his forties, would be looking for a younger model.

In their defense, I should have been more insightful and specific at the time my friends tried to play matchmaker. However, I didn't have a clue what *my type* was, until I ran across an old television rerun I use to watch as a child. There he was, Dick Van Dyke—same name, same body type, same playful nature as my late-husband. In that moment, I realized that I had a childhood crush on Dick Van Dyke and, at last, finally, knew *my type*.

I gradually discovered, as many women have, that the good ones are taken by middle age...especially in Minnesota, where the women outnumber the men. When a man becomes free, in the bold north country, he is either snatched up within a year or he goes for a younger model. And I learned that you can't be a cougar unless you have a good plastic surgeon and are financially endowed.

As a last resort, I've entertained the thought of utilizing my accompanist expertise and posting some ads at local churches. The flyer would go something like this:

For hire: Experienced organist/pianist to play at any middle-aged woman's funeral (preferably 50—59), survived by a like-aged widower who looks like Dick Van Dyke. I work **cheap.**

That way I'd find them right off the starting block.

Chapter 40

Crazy (Can't Blame It on the Cat) Ladies

My most cherished memories of my marriage were the times Dick and I would retire to our deck in the evenings. He would often savor a cold Budweiser and I would entertain my glass of wine until the sun disappeared behind the horizon and the mosquitos started their attack. The pests were mostly attracted to Dick; hence I had some reprieve.

Sometimes we would discuss politics, work or our finances, but the focus of our dialogue was mostly about Danny. Sometimes our discussions would turn into disagreements, especially pertaining to politics—Dick would often say I canceled his vote at every election. However, the atmosphere was usually serene on the deck in view of the sunset.

That must be why I still gravitated to the deck after Dick's death. It's the place I felt closest to him—barring his workbench in the garage which did not have the same reflective atmosphere. But after countless nights singing with

Josh and searching for God in the clouds, I started to tire of spending my nights alone in my own thoughts. My grief work had been tedious and redundant, because that is how it must be. But I was ready for a change. So, in Dick's absence, I started seeking acquaintances to share my deck, the ambience of the sunset, and a soft or not-so-soft drink.

This practice was eventually referred to as "drecking." Before long, I amassed an entourage of comrades and learned that I had no criteria for procuring girlfriends. They just had to like my company and my lakeshore. Mostly the latter. With time, when retreating to my deck in the evenings, my thoughts were not of Dick but of new memories which replaced the old.

Linda, my angel with metal wings, was the ultimate bleeding heart and a cat lover like myself. She was usually a two-cat family, depending on strays that ended up at her doorstep. She was methodical in her actions and words, always thinking before speaking. I should have learned from her during my transformation, but I didn't. She was married to a good man who enjoyed watching TV in the man cave of his garage. Because of this, she would head to my deck for female comradery, one sweet drink and conversation.

Connie, at first impression, appeared to be quiet and soft spoken. Unlike me, her one sentence *was* "she is *so* sweet". However, her demeanor would progressively change through the evening to be heard above my more vocal friends, and the two glasses of champagne helped a little. Hers was usually a two-cat family, depending if one would become an escapee.

April, who would mostly partake in the snacks and iced tea on my deck, once had financial security but then lost it in the 2008 recession. She endured through single parenting and entry-level jobs to become a strong, independent woman. Even though her fortune was gone, she could have been described as a diva in a different respect—her professional soprano voice was comparable to an angel.

My dear friend and neighbor, Beth would visit the deck daily, to my surprise and pleasure. That is, until she divorced her husband and moved away from the lake house next door. But I was delighted that she didn't stay away for long and continued to join us unexpectedly. She was our conversation facilitator, always ensuring that every person had a chance to speak during the group's usual competitive conversations. This dear friend was a tad quirkier than the rest—she had officially been diagnosed with a bi-polar disorder. Rarely predictable or boring, Beth was entertaining and fun to analyze with my amateur psychology degree.

Leslie had an infectious laugh, a good heart, and the tendency to swing the topic of a recipe or a movie back to politics. This was very brave of her, since most present were not in agreement with her views. She was also an accomplished artist, nanny by trade and could cook better than Rachel Ray. Her gourmet meals stopped the wine from racing to our heads.

Always the voice of reason, Kathe would listen intently and try to see all sides of an argument. Even though she would never judge another's opinion, she may question one's alleged facts. She had her irritations on politics only because she was very educated on the subject. Sometimes it's not good to know too much, I guess. Kathe was not an animal lover, until my younger cat developed a special attachment to her. Eventually, she warmed to having a feline on her lap and cat hair on her clothes.

Sue was very giving of her time and a busy volunteer for any worthy cause. She thought anyone was hilarious who laughed at their own jokes and had good stories to tell. She especially loved being entertained by Clarice.

Because Clarice was a creative person extremely busy with kids, her music director job, and rescuing elderly people and canines, she didn't always have the time to think before acting. She absolutely had some great stories, e.g. admonishing the humane society for requesting she take a drug test when they only asked if she would take a "lab."

But the queen of stories was Nora. Because she had been my roommate in college and first knew me as the "Wild Woman," we shared some interesting memories that she could expound on much better than I. Nora could run a marathon monologue, usually, without boring a single person. Her cultivated grasp of vocabulary always lent to an interesting tale. Being a tall, big-boned woman with a trace of Native American descent, Nora filled a room with her presence and her voice. It would never surprise us when she would break into song in Barbara Streisand mode. Thank goodness her voice was lovely.

After the five years it took me to graduate from college, Sandy and I met in flight attendant training. While I still served soda to the masses, unfortunately, she had to take an early retirement after thirteen surgeries on her rotator cuffs due to the hazards of our career; for example, three-hundred-pound overhead bins and five-hundred-pound beverage carts. Sandy harbored at least two cats and a dog or two at any given time. As my roommate in "stew school," we also shared some interesting stories, which are not spoken on my deck and will not be divulged here. What happens in "stew school" stays in "stew school."

Roxy was also widowed; the reason why she loved her wine as much as I did. And the timbre of her laugh equaled Leslie's. At 71, she was in marathon shape and spent every day exercising in some mode, from kettle bells to yoga. She often needed to get home before dark because her mode of transportation was usually a bike.

Kitty was a teetotaler who had as much fun as the imbibers. She was comfortable being center stage, as was I, therefore, at times we couldn't resist entertaining the troupes together with a song or dance. To our dismay, she did not frequent the deck as often after finding a wonderful man to marry. Consequently, I discovered that the show couldn't go on without her, because a solo act merely appeared like a crazy lady on too much wine. Kitty had an attack cat until the husband came into the picture. Unfortunately, the naughty feline didn't protect the house but preferred to terrorize my friend. Bye, bye, Kitty's kitty.

Always to our delight, my 85-year-old neighbor would often saunter over from her yard in her knit pants and slippers while carrying her tiny glass of wine, which more resembled a thimble. Standing up to five feet on her tiptoes, Lily delighted us with her many army wife stories. It was encouraging to me that she still mowed her own lawn—with a *push* lawn mower—but mostly, still enjoyed her wine. She didn't like my felines, therefore, they consistently tried to win her affection.

On occasion a random male friend, husband or young children would visit my deck. Although, these genres were usually not invited with my crazy ladies in the evenings. I had no prejudice against males nor children but preferred to preserve the dynamics of the female conversation. I imagine there would have been less divulging...and probably less cussing for sure. Not cussing in the normal sense of the word, but, what I would refer to as, *passive* cursing. While never using the F-word, Jesus or God attached to any profanity, one friend could creatively apply "shit" and "damn" as adjectives and prepositions in the same sentence.

And, of course, canines were never allowed. No one wanted two frightened, traumatized kitties on the deck.

My ladies and I would sometimes move from "drecking" to the floaties, which I had permanently anchored in the water with a cement block. Thankfully, I didn't sell that for a buck in a garage sale. Of course, each floatie had a cup holder for our soft- or not-so-soft-drinks, and so our pastime was dubbed "flinking." When we tired of floating aimlessly atop the waves, we moved to our chairs in the shallow water where we would enjoy "sinking" until the sun started to set. As the air turned cooler, we would move back to the deck and continue "drecking" until the mosquitos appeared, Roxy had to bike home, Leslie's food ran out, Clarice or Nora ran out of stories, or Sue got tired of laughing at them.

For years, we had many memorable gatherings when we would attempt to solve world problems and share our accomplishments or woes of the day. This abridged list of comrades ranged from 23 years my senior to 18 years my junior, and were married, widowed, divorced, divorced many times, politically right to left, religious to atheist, from cat lovers and dog lovers to animal abiders, in charge of young kids and teenagers or having multiple grandkids. Despite our differences, my entourage of friends and I had a few things in common: no one was afraid to express her opinion, and we collectively got a little quirkier with each meeting on my deck.

I always appreciated the comradery my ladies gave me, but their true gift was so much more. They knew me well and still kind of liked me. Isn't that what happens when people grow older together?

Chapter 41

Christmas Letters and a Crutch

I'm sure my family and friends thought that my interest in dating indicated that I was "getting better," which I was. But, of course, bereavement has no end date. One doesn't "get better" as if you have a virus or bacterial infection. That's why a bereavement card can never be late. You'll never see a "Sorry I missed your grief" Hallmark card.

Also, the adage "it takes time to heal" is not entirely correct. Because time, in and of itself, does not heal; it merely *takes time* to do the grief work. As the grief work is tediously and painfully being accomplished, old memories are gradually replaced with new ones.

I think I started healing when I took Dick's voice off our voice mail—or maybe the healing came first and moved me to action.

By the time Danny graduated from Notre Dame in 2010, I had found enjoyment in Christmas again. I had stopped feeling the need to watch *Christmas Vacation* in Dick's memory, and my Christmas tree returned to a Fraser fir with new ornaments symbolizing a new life.

The cheery Christmas letters *almost* stopped bothering me...but not quite. Ultimately, I decided to do what I do best, put my thoughts down on paper. I designed my first Christmas letter and mailed it to three of my closest friends. Because they were going through some crappy things at the time, it was well received. It went something like this:

Happy Holidays to all!

Danny and I had quite an exciting year! After a forty percent pay cut at my airline job in January, I was able to find a third church job to make up for the increase in our property taxes. We are so blessed!

After my bout of shingles dissipated in March, things started to look up, and Easter was celebrated with a family gathering! Even though my influenza and Danny's mono were an inconvenience, soon summer arrived, and the weather was cooperative at the lake. Our lovely view of Cooks Bay was further enhanced after I cleared the fallen willow tree which had crushed our roof during the big tornado. I love my chainsaw!

The floor boards dried up nicely after the flood in June, so Danny and I finally decided to purchase Velcro shades for our windows. We were both excited that my wedding dress and china sold on Craigslist to make that happen! Life is good!

Even though a family vacation was not financially in the cards for us in August, we took many memorable trips to Dick's, Billy's, Suzie's, and Grandma Helen's gravesites. (Pictures on the back!)

Despite the empty seat at the table after the passing

*of Grandpa Frank, our family's Thanksgiving was full
of love and thankfulness. Especially after a cousin left in
a fit of anger, peace and comradery was upon us all!*

Christmas Cheer from our house to yours!

*Love, The Devenys
(Please excuse the stained paper, roof will be fixed
soon!)*

Honestly, the letter was part exaggeration, but the
parody was very much enjoyed by my friends and cathartic
for me. Once again, I will emphasize: *Do not* send cheery
Christmas letters with pictures of complete families to the
newly bereaved.

Instead of eavesdropping on adolescent poker games
with self-pity on New Year's Eve, I decided to have a party of
my own. My friends and I were quickly advancing in years,
so I thought it appropriate to have a 1st Annual "Old
L'Anxiety" Party. The name was fitting because the party
started at 5:00 and the countdown was at 9:00. In church-
lady fashion, we played the dice game with our Christmas
white elephant gifts as prizes.

By that time, Valentine's Day became a nonevent, and I
stopped buying presents in the name of my husband and
merely enjoyed the flowers my son would reliably send.

Instead of frequenting Dick's grave on every holiday, I
started placing perennials there on Memorial Day and
refrained from venturing to it in the frigid winter. As with
Billy's grave, I found the need to visit had dwindled with
time, and I could honor Dick's memory in other ways. The
symbolisms of the past were not needed anymore.

Soon Barry, my handyman whom I used to the extent of

his benevolence, became unavailable for my toilet repairs. After frantically searching for a new rescuer, I procured a six-foot-six Adonis named Bruce, whom I deemed "Bruce the Almighty." Not just a reliable handyman, but eye candy as well.

It's true that my transformation had not quite created that "sweet" JoAnn whom I should have become. An outsider may even say I became hardened through my adversities, but that's not entirely true. While I tended to underplay the trivial circumstances in life, I also felt a deeper empathy for those going through monumental trials.

After all my advancements, I still couldn't shake the initial jealousy and abysmal emptiness when viewing the dynamics of complete families. That completeness and sense of belonging, which I once took for granted, had become an endeared memory. But its memory also accentuated the void of its absence.

However, when I would fall into these grips of self-absorption, I would imagine the people who had never had a husband, siblings, or children; those who had never known belonging. Had I never known the completeness of family, would I miss it so much now? Of course not. But had I not experienced it at all, I would have missed so much. My life had been merciless at times, but it had also been enriched by a supportive family, my son, crazy ladies, a stand-in dad, and the odd random date.

You could say Dick and I still had a relationship, only it was changed. When I would talk to him, he seemed to be nearer. But the fact that he didn't talk back was a mixed blessing or a disappointment. I missed his touch, his laughter, his playfulness, and even our heated conversations. But I knew I'd see him again. You see, I struggled with my faith in its details, but never my beliefs. Even though I believed that God could have prevented my losses but chose to allow them, he had also walked me through hell and back. "Shit" happened, and while I was wallowing through it, God prevented me from getting stuck.

My atheist friend would probably say that faith was a crutch for me...and I would agree: He was a crutch when I couldn't walk, my sail when I couldn't stay afloat, my life preserver when I was drowning, and my wings when I was ready to fly. Because of my "crutch," I had plodded through the crap and had arrived at that place called acceptance. There was some kind of peace in that.

Chapter 42

Confessions:
Mowing Forward

The engine sputtered on the second pull, but I wasn't concerned because, typically, Dick's forty-year-old Toro would hold out until the fourth. It was 2012, Dick had been gone for ten years, and the lawn mower was still running on merely gas and absolutely no maintenance. It could only have been divine intervention.

Consistent with tradition, it roared on the fourth pull, and black smoke billowed from the engine. *Does a lawn mower need oil?* I wondered.

Outside work was cathartic for me—versus domestic that is—and my mind wandered while nudging the mower over the many invasive roots from the neighbor's poplar tree.

I watched as the grass was swallowed by the ancient beast and noticed that the vibrant green was mottled with differing textures of crabgrass and creeping-charlie. Both arrived the summer after Dick's departure, and he, of course, would never have allowed their intrusion. While he was a purist when it came to his lawn, consequently I had spent the last ten years digging up his cherished sod to make my flower beds. However, with every shovel load of dirt, every overfilled wheelbarrow, and every new plant introduced to the soil, I had done my best reminiscing. You could say that the perennial gardens had been fertilized with memories and watered with tears.

If grief is an energy, it can't just disappear, it must go somewhere. I pondered this while the mower severed the heads off the clover in front of me. *Maybe my grief energy was turned in, and now it's turned out.* Heading to the front yard challenge, I muscled the machine across the surface of river rock I had laid over the dirt at the side of the house. It was an area shaded by our ancient willow, and even Dick could not make the grass grow there.

While propelling around the roots of our majestic elm tree and staring at the dandelions in my path, I suddenly realized I had been brazenly singing out loud. It was reminiscent of those nights on my deck after Dick's death when I was searching for God in the clouds. However, the song I inadvertently caught myself singing wasn't one of Josh Groban's—I had overused his songs by that time. When realizing the words, I stopped mowing and released the handle, causing the engine to gasp into silence.

Because the neighbors already knew, as a widow, I talked and sang to myself, I allowed myself a hearty gut laugh right in the middle of my miniscule front yard. There was something pathetic and, at the same time, amusing in the fact that I had been singing Billy Joel's "*I Love You Just the Way You Are*"...to my lawn. Sometimes you can do nothing else to make things better but to chuckle.

So that's what I had learned to do: find humor in the

challenges, identify a positive to the hardships. Or maybe I was striving toward the ordinary, and by that, moving away from tragedy. After my transformation, I would joke about my husband or his death at times, hoping that other widows were not offended. It's not as if I didn't love my husband, it was just my way of humanizing him.

God, I know you understand. With all that transpires down here, there really must be someone up there with a sense of humor.

Bringing my thoughts back to the job at hand, I pulled the cord on the old Toro and it sputtered.

Epilogue

Perception and the Colors of Healing

The sky is darkening, and the sun casts a fragmented orange glow over the reflective blue ice. But my gaze is set on the task before me. My gloved hands grip the shovel while my skates' momentum propel it back and forth between the snow-piled boundaries of the covered ice. *Yes, I know how to shovel a rink without your instructions, Mr. New York City.*

Even though Danny and his friends have stopped using the rink, I maintain it throughout winter. Consequently, the accumulated hours I spend shoveling far outweighs its usage. However, I much prefer the strenuous, outdoor activity versus joining a health club. Remaining stationary on an elliptical bike is not as rewarding as the progressive clearing of snow from the luminescent ice. Like the summer, when my most insightful thinking is from my deck above the glow of the sunset, reflective moments are also found eye-level with the horizon on the frozen lake of the winter.

Out of exhaustion, I pause from shoveling to catch my

breath. When gasping in the crisp air, I feel its coolness down my throat, and then with its escape, it becomes a lingering mist. There is a void of sound, an unusual silence, except for a faint snowmobile engine from a distant bay or an occasional drop of icicle from a branch of a tree onto the soft snow. I focus on the red ball of the sunset and notice that the colors of the clouds are more vivid in the dead of winter than they had been in the warm summer skies.

I sometimes miss the days when I searched for God in the clouds, because I once found comfort in it. But by the time the clouds got harder to see, I had found what I was looking for. In any case, it was probably futile to look for God in the distance, because he eventually became the strength within me. So near.

Now I've come to see the clouds quite differently. I see them like an inverted picture, where a person may see two faces while focusing on one color yet see a lamp when focusing on the other. The sky is more prominent versus the grayish white clouds, so I see a different image. It's the brightness behind the clouds that allowed me to see the most. Life is like that inverted picture—I can choose to see the clouds, or I can eventually concentrate on the light behind them. It's all about perception.

In my lifetime, I have seen many perfectly cloudless skies where the blue is strikingly vivid. Beautiful in its own way, but not a scene a painter would paint on canvas or a photographer would want to capture on film. A perfectly blue sky has no depth. Yet, many artists have painted and photographed sunsets framed by the contrast of multi-hued clouds. It's the contrast of the clouds against the blue that makes the sky beautiful, and they only portray their colors when light is shining through them.

Until you've stepped out of a wet swimsuit, how can you

appreciate dry clothes? If you have never cried, how do you really savor a guttural laugh? Until you've lost, how can you really appreciate your loved ones? And when the sky does not have one cloud, how can you see God?

The sun is slowly vanishing, so I turn my back to the dark skies and skate toward the shore. I navigate the yard by the bright, amber glow shining through the windows of my home and anticipate its comforting warmth after a cold chill.

The Devenys

1985

July 3
1987

July 1990

October 1990
Dick & Billy

January 1991

July 1991
9 days before
Billy's death

April 1991
Dick & Billy

March 2002

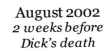

August 2002
2 weeks before
Dick's death

September 2013

2017

About the Author

Award-Winning Author, JoAnn Kuzma Deveny grew up in Hibbing, Minnesota and graduated with a Liberal Arts degree from the University of Minnesota. JoAnn has appeared on *Fox National News, the WCCO Morning Show, the KQRS Morning Show, KTIS 98.5, Rudy Maxa's World* and other media events commenting on *When Bluebirds Fly: Losing a Child, Living with Hope,* as well as her humorous air travel book, *99 Ways to Make a Flight Attendant Fly— Off the Handle!* She has appeared in featured articles in *US News & World Report, Parenting Magazine,* and additional publications.

JoAnn resides in her lake home in Mound, Minnesota and continues her flying career. On weekends, she is an accompanist for church services.

To JoAnn's delight her son, Danny, lives twenty minutes away. He is an attorney by profession.

To order the newest revisions of JoAnn's books,
please visit her website at:

www.joanndeveny.com